I0793620

A Brief History of

MOUNT DORA

FLORIDA

A Brief History of
MOUNT DORA
FLORIDA

Gary McKechnie and Nancy Howell

Foreword by Gilbert King

THE History PRESS

Published by The History Press
Charleston, SC
www.historypress.net

Cover images: Donnelly House and lighthouse photos by Nancy Howell. Football team image courtesy of the Mount Dora Historical Society.

First published 2016

Manufactured in the United States

ISBN 978.1.46711.842.2

Library of Congress Control Number: 2015954749

This book is dedicated to historian and author James Laux, whose research and published works offer invaluable insights to Mount Dora's past.

It is also dedicated to Dave Felts, past president of the Mount Dora Historical Society and founding chairman of the Mount Dora Historic Preservation Board. He continues to be a primary source of information regarding Mount Dora's history and deserves credit for his role in saving valuable landmarks.

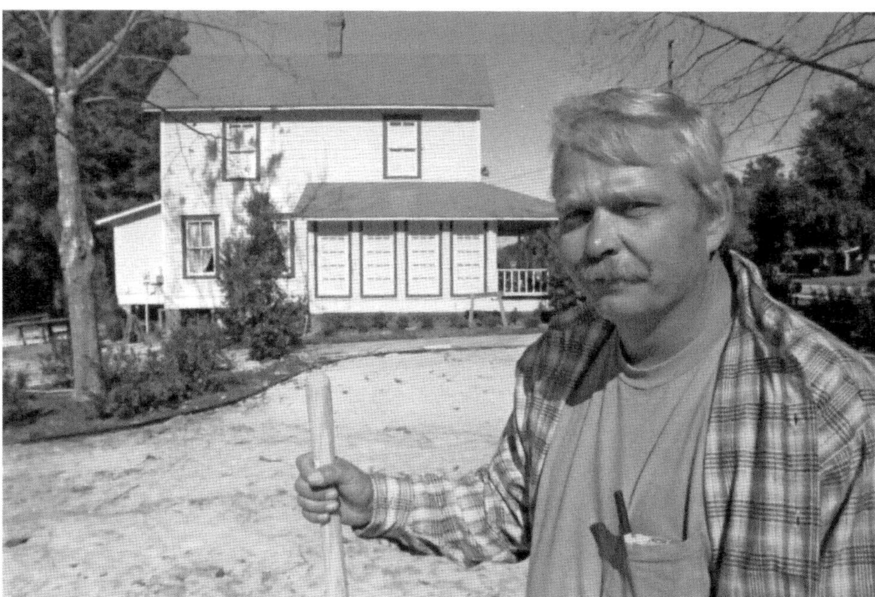

Dave Felts. *Mount Dora Historical Society.*

CONTENTS

FOREWORD

I won't ever forget the first time I drove into Mount Dora. I'd spent quite a bit of time in Lake County, from Groveland to Tavares to Leesburg, and one afternoon I found myself driving down Donnelly Street into the heart of this little city where oak trees lined the sidewalks and colorful awnings adorned quaint shops. "There has to be a story behind this place," I remember thinking at the time. It was like no other place I'd been to in Lake County.

Sure enough, there are quite a few stories behind Mount Dora, and Gary McKechnie and Nancy Howell have it all right here in this fun and highly accessible book. From the history of its earliest settlers (including Annie and J.P. Donnelly) to Mabel Norris Reese (the famed editor of the *Mount Dora Topic*) to the filming of the infamous and star-studded *Honky Tonk Freeway*, Gary and Nancy truly capture the beauty and quirkiness of this gem of a central Florida city.

Anyone who's ever been to Mount Dora knows that they've been to a special place in Lake County, and this book is a worthy and indispensable look at the city's culture, history, politics and, most importantly, its charm.

Gilbert King
October 2015

PREFACE

Even if an event happened five thousand years ago, its effects never really diminish. There will always be new information, another discovery or a different interpretation that changes the way we understand what happened all those years ago. The same is true with the ongoing history of Mount Dora. Often rumors become stories, then stories become legends and, finally, legends become facts. Thankfully, researchers and historians dig for truth the same as prospectors dig for gold.

Having lived in Mount Dora since 1992, we gained a better sense of the community by becoming deeply involved with the chamber of commerce, the Mount Dora Historical Society, the Library Association, the music festival, city council meetings, committees and other civic and nonprofit associations. Through our participation, we acquired a fairly good sense of the town's recent history and added another layer of historical awareness through friendships and conversations with Mount Dora natives and longtime residents.

For events preceding our arrival, we turned to historians and authors who shared a desire to chronicle—and sometimes correct—the tales from Mount Dora's past. Much of the information you'll read was found in *The Story of Mount Dora, Florida*, written by R.J. Longstreet in 1960. The book was a project of the Mount Dora Historical Society that, in large part, was formed to produce a work that gathered the historic highlights of the town as well as applaud the people who played a role in Mount Dora's creation.

Other sources include James Laux's well-researched book *A Short History of Mount Dora, Florida* (2001); *Memories of Mount Dora and Lake County: 1845 to*

1981, by David Edgerton (1983); Vivian Owens's *The Mount Dorans* (2001); *Mount Dora: The Rest of the Story, Plus!*, by Reverend Eugene Burley (2000); and Judy Pendleton's *The Lakeside Inn* (1998). Thanks to their efforts, *Brief History of Mount Dora, Florida* had a head start with a wealth of material that looked at similar events, but almost always from a different perspective.

The Mount Dora Historical Society's archives, housed at the W.T. Bland Public Library, provided additional insights through articles, photographs, pamphlets, papers and assorted ephemera. Seventy years of the local newspaper, the *Mount Dora Topic*, are preserved on microfilm at the Eustis Memorial Library. Those volumes proved to be an indispensable source of information and led to one conclusion.

Mount Dora is a small town with a big history.

For additional information, images and stories related to *A Brief History of Mount Dora, Florida*, visit:

www.mountdorahistory.com

ACKNOWLEDGEMENTS

In addition to the authors of the aforementioned works, we extend our gratitude to Jane Trimble, Steve Williams, Patti Wightman, Darlin Berry, William Sievert, David Cohea, Beth Forbes, Jim Clark and Gilbert King. We also appreciate the assistance of Carolyn Green and the Mount Dora Historical Society, the Lake County Historical Society, the W.T. Bland Public Library, the Eustis Memorial Library and the State Library and Archives of Florida.

INTRODUCTION

Mount Dora. Today, the town appears to be running on cruise control as locals, weekenders and snowbirds filter into the downtown historic shopping village to hunt for art and antiques; check out the latest fashions; relax at a day spa; and sample beers, wines, coffees, teas, foods and desserts at cozy pubs, eateries, sidewalk cafés and award-winning restaurants. You can crack open a good book at an honest-to-goodness independent bookstore, settle back for a concert and, quite often, join tens of thousands of festival-goers celebrating art, music, crafts, collectibles, antiques, plants, food, bicycles…or anything else residents believe deserves a celebration.

Radiating out from the shopping village, neighborhoods reflect an eclectic quilt of architectural styles ranging from charming boathouses turned rustic residences to 1920s vintage cottages, 1950s ranch ramblers, Victorian homes and lakefront mansions. Speedboats, sailboats, catamarans and pontoon boats glide across 4,475-acre Lake Dora, often under the watchful eyes of red-tailed hawks, egrets, herons, bald eagles and curious alligators. Walk along the shoreline and you will find families picnicking in Gilbert Park, visitors exploring the waterfront boardwalk, people snapping photos of an adorable inland lighthouse and nature lovers admiring some of the most majestic sunsets in Florida.

Follow the walkway to the Lawn Bowling Club and historic Lakeside Inn and, beyond that, to the state's oldest inland yacht club and you will notice that the town is full of activity. In the village, there's a steady schedule of tennis and pickleball, as well as concerts on the lawn, movies in the park, art gallery openings and merchants hosting after-hour events. Musicians serenade diners at outdoor cafés, couples savor fine foods and wines and groups gather with their puppies at pet-friendly socials. Walk around the town after sunset and you will hear sounds of cheering crowds at high school football games and tent revivalists praising a preacher's sermon, as well as the long, eerie call of hoot owls floating through the evening air.

MOUNT DORA, USA

Located in Florida's midsection, Mount Dora is essentially Middle America—a town of thirteen thousand that has settled into a comfortable balance. Geographically, it is almost equidistant between the Atlantic Ocean and the Gulf of Mexico, although its southern charm may stem from it being closer to Georgia than to Miami.

The town boasts the impressive distinction of having one of the highest elevations in Florida: 184 feet above sea level. This fact encourages the proliferation of "I Climbed Mount Dora" T-shirts, but don't tell anyone that there is no mountain to climb. Temperatures in the summer average around 80 degrees (although it feels like 120), and in the winter it drops to around 58 degrees (although it feels like 80). There are a dozen parks that the city dubs "major" and nine smaller parks that it places in the minor leagues.

Mount Dora residents are young and old, aspiring and affluent. Demographically, it's a mix of white (63.9 percent), black (18.4 percent), Hispanic (13.3 percent) and Asian (2.5 percent). Just over half of its residents are female (54.3 percent). In 2013, the median age was 44.5, and the median income was $46,925, slightly ahead of the state average. There is a solid base of conservatives and a rapidly growing number of liberals. Volunteers donate thousands of hours to nonprofits and charities and actively participate in a range of civic, social and fraternal clubs.

Between Third Avenue and Eleventh Avenue and from Clayton Street to Helen Street, the entire Mount Dora Historic District is listed on the National Register of Historic Places.

There are few towns in Florida like Mount Dora. Here's a brief history of how it got that way.

Chapter 1

THE MIDDLE OF NOWHERE

Something gnawing at the kitchen door after we retire at night...
—Mount Dora resident

Clearing the Way

It's doubtful you ever think about what happens to your trash once it leaves your home. But if any of those items happen to have a long shelf life, someday a far distant generation of archaeologists may likely be fascinated by your dead flip phone, broken VHS player and thermal paper fax machine.

Piecing together the past from discarded materials is what happened when archaeologists scouring Lake County found communal dumping grounds called middens. Buried within them, shell beads, arrowheads, shards of broken pottery and the charred remains of long-extinguished campfires revealed that the land surrounding what would become Mount Dora had been visited by members of the Timucua tribe roughly five hundred years ago. Researchers also unearthed pieces of European-made items, hinting that tribes had traded with early Spanish explorers, although there's no evidence that the Spaniards, Timucuas or any other tribe ever established a permanent residence here.

Of course, if any Indians *had* settled here, chances are they would have been, let's say, "encouraged" to leave in the mid-1830s, when General Abraham Eustis arrived during the Second Seminole War. His mission: To clear the area of Native Americans. If they didn't get the message then, a year later they would have when a battalion of Alabama volunteers arrived in support of General Eustis.

Pitching their tents east of what would become Mount Dora, these soldiers camped out in a relatively mysterious region of Florida. But neither the soldiers nor the Indians they were pursuing would stay. So aside from a body of water (Lake Eustis) and a neighboring town (Eustis) later named for the general, this section of Florida had little permanence at the time.

That was about to change, and quickly. Over the next several decades, determined homesteaders would head into the Florida wilderness, where they would chop down pines, put up cabins and stake their claims in the sticky, mosquito-infested middle of nowhere. Over the years, a number of settlements would either flourish or fade. Among them were Fort Mason, Ravenswood, Slighville, Lake Griffin, Leesburg, Pittman, Yalaha, Lisbon, Acron…and Mount Dora.

Home, Sweet Homestead

It's hard to imagine why anyone would have wanted to come to this hot and humid area in the mid-1800s*, but there was something more enticing than physical comfort. There was land—lots of it.

The end of the Second Seminole War would position Florida for major change. By 1842, the government had either chased thousands of Native Americans into the reeds and waters of the Everglades or forced them to march one thousand miles to the Oklahoma Territory. In the wake of their involuntary absence, there was an increased incentive to populate the now Indian-free territory with anyone who was white. As far as Congress was concerned, the best way to accomplish this was to pass the Florida Armed Occupation Act of 1842. This policy offered 160 acres to any "head of the family," usually a man, who would bear arms to protect the area against potential renewed hostilities, build a

**Decades later, when the town was arguably much more livable, one resident wrote to a friend about "the alligators in the backyard, snakes fighting in the orange groves, lizards racing back and forth across the tea towel line over the kitchen stove catching flies—yes, and something gnawing at the kitchen door after we retire at night."*

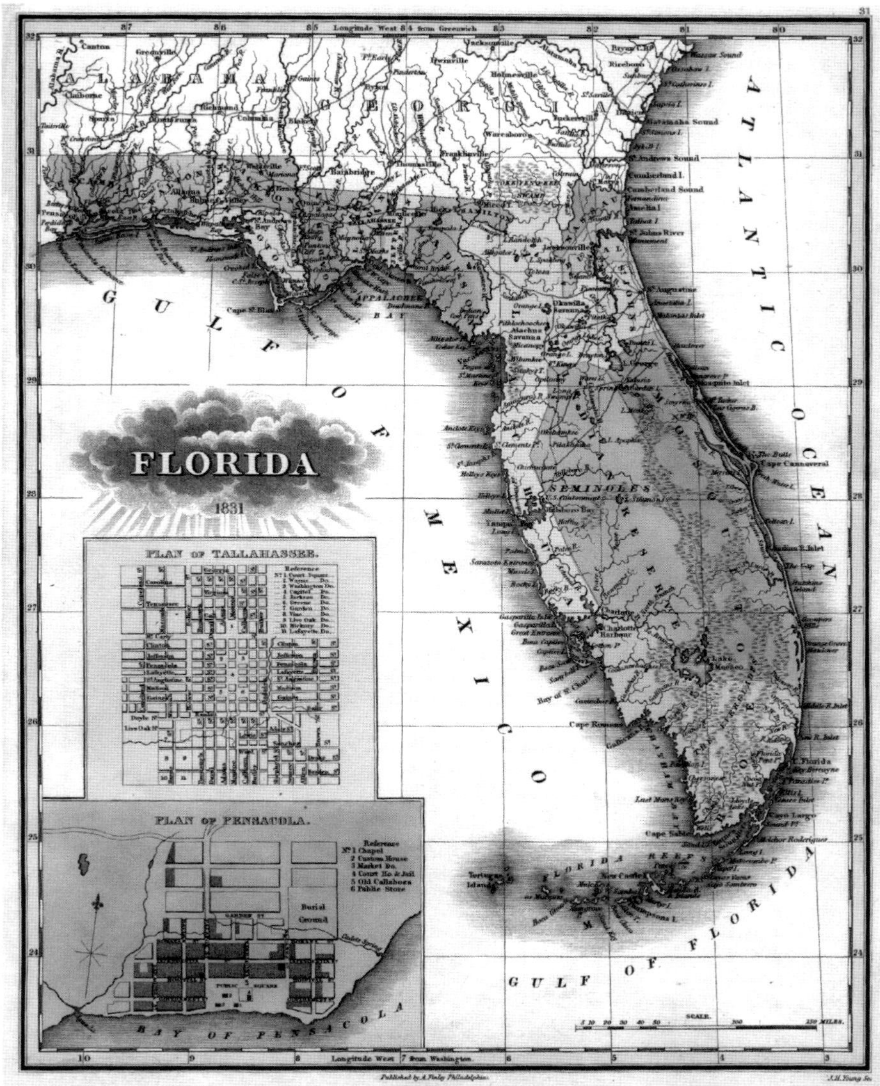

Florida's interior was a mystery to most in 1831. By the mid-1840s, it had attracted thousands of homesteaders when Florida achieved statehood. *Mount Dora Historical Society.*

habitable dwelling within two miles of a garrisoned military post, enclose and cultivate at least 5 acres of the land and live on the property for at least five years.

In March 1845, when Florida achieved statehood, things took a major leap forward. This was no longer a simple territory; it was the nation's twenty-seventh state, and the federal government became increasingly determined to develop the land. Maps of the time showed that the region south of the Florida Panhandle was nearly empty. It was an unexplored wilderness ready to be tamed.

Chapter 2

WHAT BECOMES A LEGEND MOST

When the legend becomes fact, print the legend.
—The Man Who Shot Liberty Valance

The Legend, Part I

Should you visit Mount Dora for more than a day, at some point you'll run across a local who will corner you and share the story of Dora Ann Drawdy. According to legend, the twenty-year-old and her husband, James, received word that they could homestead 160 acres in Florida. Up to the task, they left Irwin County, Georgia, and headed south.

Their story, as passed through family history, was recounted in 1974 by the Drawdys' then eighty-three-year-old granddaughter, May Tucker Lynn. As Lynn recalled, the family, including a grandmother and three children, loaded up a wagon and ox cart packed with farming tools and supplies and began their long journey from Georgia to, well, somewhere. Sticking to trails as often as possible, when they reached what should have been an insurmountable obstacle in Florida's Big Bend, the Drawdys displayed no shortage of gumption. Rather than turn back, they chopped down trees, built rafts and ferried their wagons and livestock across the Suwannee River. Setting out again from the opposite shore, the family continued heading south, with Dora on foot ahead of the wagon to keep their livestock from straying.

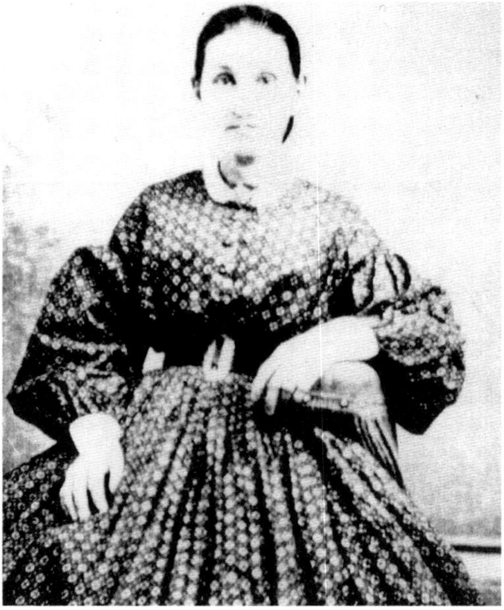
Dora Ann Drawdy, the woman many people believe inspired the name of the town. *City of Mount Dora.*

Several weeks later, they reached a point between two magnificent lakes where they parked their wagon and settled in. Industrious and enterprising, the family staked out their spread, cut down pine trees to build a log cabin and then chopped down saplings to create corrals for their hogs and cattle and chickens. They began growing grapefruit trees (which they claimed were the first in Florida), ran a cotton gin, wove thread into clothing and cured hides into leather to make shoes.

According to family history, the Drawdy family matriarch would soon lend her name to history.

The Legend, Part II

In 1846, surveying crews were sent across Florida to map the land. With nearly sixty-six thousand square miles of state to cover, this would be an arduous task. After Florida achieved statehood, surveyor C.C. Tracy arrived in what would become Mount Dora to run the boundary lines. He noted the "third rate open rolling pine," a "waggon course road" and then a marsh, a "hammock" and "the shore of a large lake."

Picking up where Tracy left off, a three-man team arrived two years later to complete a more detailed map of the area. In December 1848, deputy surveyor James A. Gould along with chainmen Demetrio Solana and Domingo Pacetty worked their way across the wilderness. The only trace of human activity was a trail—perhaps one created by General Eustis during the war—that skirted the edge of the 4,475-acre lake that Tracy had seen. Hauling their chains and equipment south, they pressed on until they

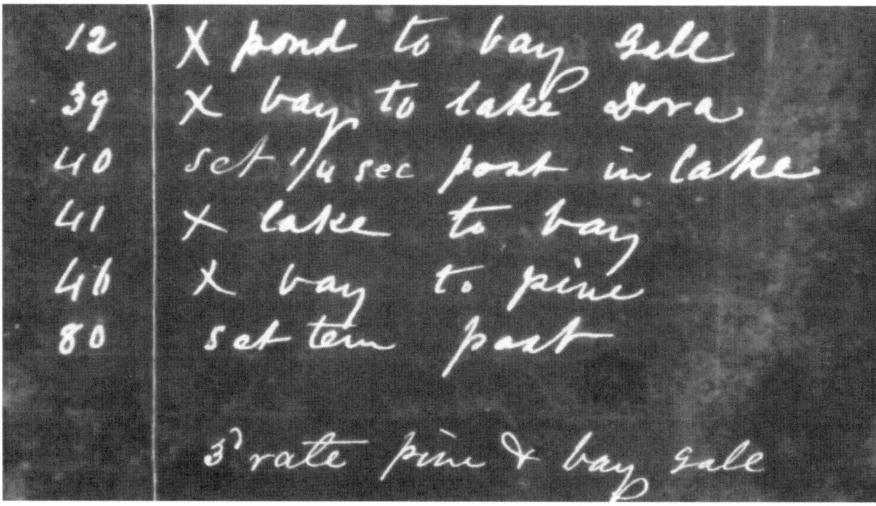
12 X pond to bay gale
39 X bay to lake Dora
40 set 1/4 sec post in lake
41 X lake to bay
46 X bay to pine
80 set tem post

3d rate pine & bay gale

Above: Notes from Gould's survey of the area in which Lake Dora is mentioned were a key part of the Dora Drawdy legend. *Mount Dora Historical Society.*

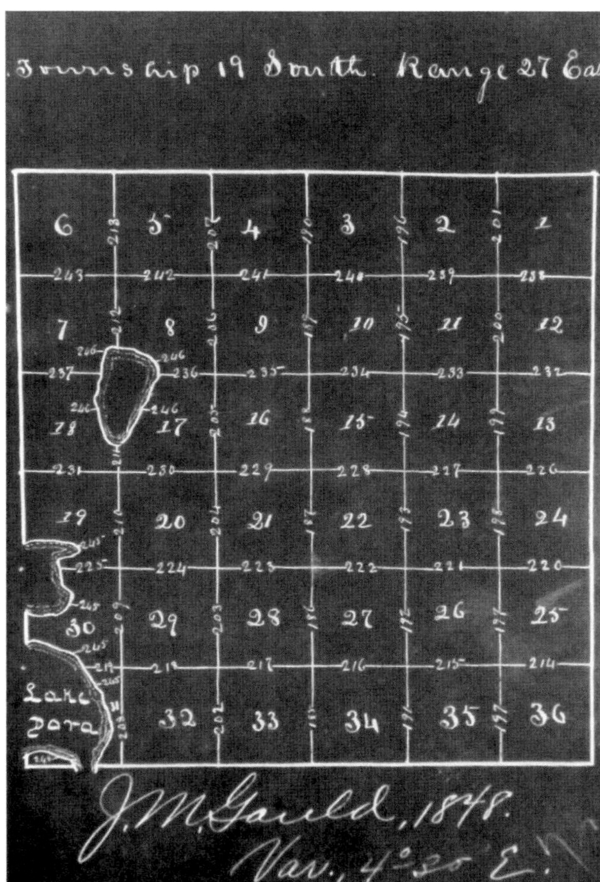

Right: Gould's 1848 diagram of the area shows "Lake Dora" at the lower left. As historian Walter Sime discovered, the name predates the arrival of the Drawdy family. *Mount Dora Historical Society.*

arrived at a channel leading to a second lake. Before them they spied a cabin, a corral and a family.

The Drawdys, likely delighted to have company, invited the surveyors to set up camp on their land. Each day, after running chains and mapping the area, the surveyors would return to their headquarters and visit with the neighboring family. "My grandmother gave them meals and did their laundry," recalled Lynn. "When they sent their report to Washington, the large lake they named Lake Dora to honor my grandmother for her kindness and courtesy." Lynn's memory appears to jibe with notes from Gould's survey in which he wrote:

> *12 x to bay gall*
> *39 x bay gall to lake Dora**

Case closed? Well, it's funny you should ask.

All in the Family

Did Dora Ann Drawdy's southern hospitality *really* inspire the naming of the lake? If so, was Mount Dora named for her as well? In his book *Mount Dora, Florida: A Short History*, author James Laux cited fellow historian Walter Sime, whose research for *About Some Lakes and More in Lake County* (1995) goes a long way in dismantling the high-value legend. Poring over census reports and genealogical records, Sime found that Dora was married twice—first to James Drawdy, who left her a widow with three children when he died in Georgia in 1848, and second to James's cousin William on September 13, 1849. The first hard *written* evidence that William and Dora Drawdy and their children were living in Florida in the 1850s was an 1860 census that showed they had settled on the shores of Lake Beauclair with their eight children.

Even more revealing, Sime learned that the lake had been christened "Dora" as early as 1846 (likely by C.C. Tracy), which was several years *before* the Drawdys arrived. But even if it were Dora and William (not James) Drawdy who settled the land between lakes Beauclair and Dora,

**Gould's shorthand translates into number of chain lengths (each chain was sixty-six feet); "x" means crossed, and a "bay gall" is a swampy land overgrown with inkberry and bay trees.*

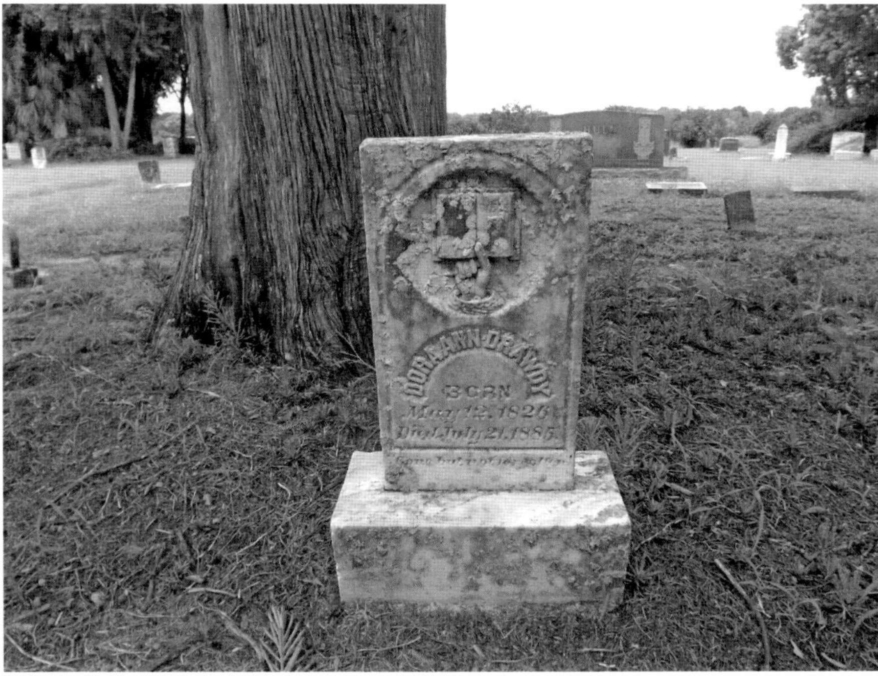

Dora Ann Drawdy is at rest in the Umatilla Cemetery. *Nancy Howell.*

the couple does deserve credit for trying to eke out a living in this new frontier. And while no one can be certain of exactly when they arrived, historians have a rough idea of when they left. That likely happened in 1861, not long after the rebels fired on Fort Sumter. With a new nation to defend, Georgia-born William Drawdy joined Florida's Eighth Infantry and headed north to fight for the Confederacy in Manassas, Harper's Ferry, Sharpsburg, Chancellorsville and Fredericksburg, where he was reportedly killed in December 1862.

Back in Florida, Dora faced the challenge of raising eight children in an isolated area. Aware that she might have to protect them from deserters and runaway slaves, she and her children moved roughly six miles northeast to a settlement called Seneca, where the two-time widow lived out her life. While it may have been coincidence that Dora happened to settle near a lake that bore her name, her tombstone was chiseled with prescient accuracy:

Dora Ann Drawdy
May 12, 1826–July 21, 1885
Gone but Not Forgotten

The Civil War claimed the life of William and changed the life of Dora Ann Drawdy. The war's aftermath would also change the fate of Florida and lead to the founding of Mount Dora.

Chapter 3

SETTLE DOWN NOW

Mount Dora is a veritable paradise.

–A.H. Cook

Home, Sweet Homestead

For Confederate soldiers who had just fought in the Civil War, returning home to what Margaret Mitchell called "a Civilization gone with the wind" could be as challenging as any battle. There was a good chance that the widespread destruction encountered along the way suggested there was most likely no home to return to. But that would soon change. The following year, hope was on the way for Confederate veterans courtesy of their former enemy: the United States government.

With the passage of the Southern Homestead Act of 1866, thousands of veterans, sharecroppers, former slaves and tenant farmers were given an opportunity for a fresh start. With federal assistance, "free Blacks and loyal Whites" could help themselves and their nation by settling 46 million acres of public land that the government had opened across the southern states. Similar to the Armed Occupation Act of 1842, the offer was simple: in exchange for living on the land and improving it, after five years a settler would acquire full ownership of 160 acres. During the tumultuous period of Reconstruction, this spelled opportunity. Florida's vast undeveloped interior provided a refuge for Confederate veterans, and thousands of gritty, determined settlers found

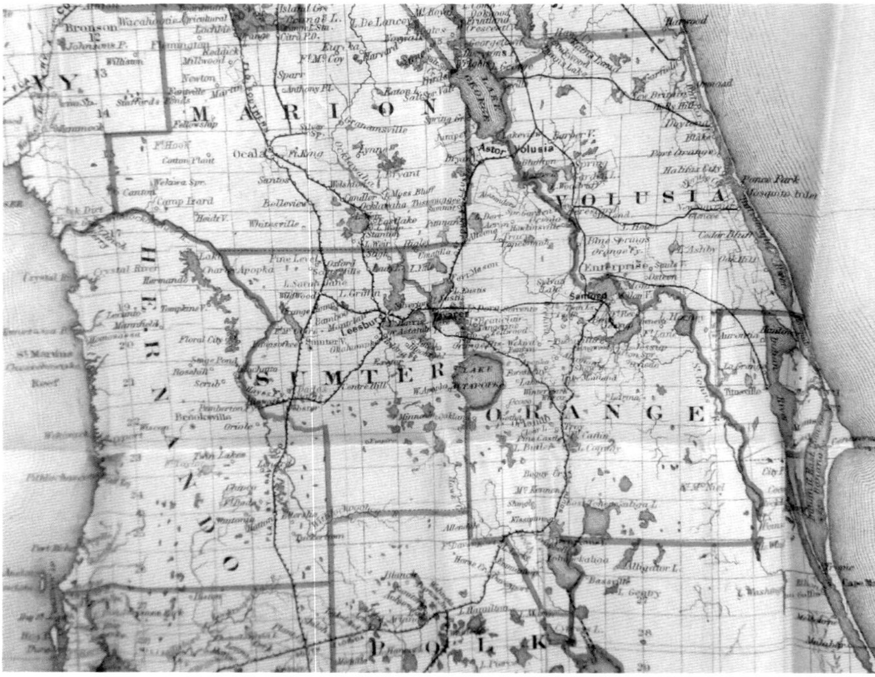

Before 1887, Lake County didn't exist. It would be carved out of sections of neighboring Sumter and Orange Counties. *Mount Dora Historical Society.*

themselves traversing gray, sandy trails and pushing their way through swamps and past longleaf pines. To their surprise, Union soldiers were also interested in the chance to stake their claim. As a result, settlers from across the reunited states began making their way to central Florida.

An area map sanctioned by Orange County commissioners after the war revealed this to be a region of promise. There was a trail connecting Sorrento and Pendryville (later Eustis), a new grade planned for a railroad and already a scattering of fledgling communities, although many would fade away. But something interesting was about to happen not far from the land the Drawdys had left.

The Simpsons

For plantation owners in the South, the years following the Civil War had not been good for business. In the wake of Lincoln's death and the ensuing

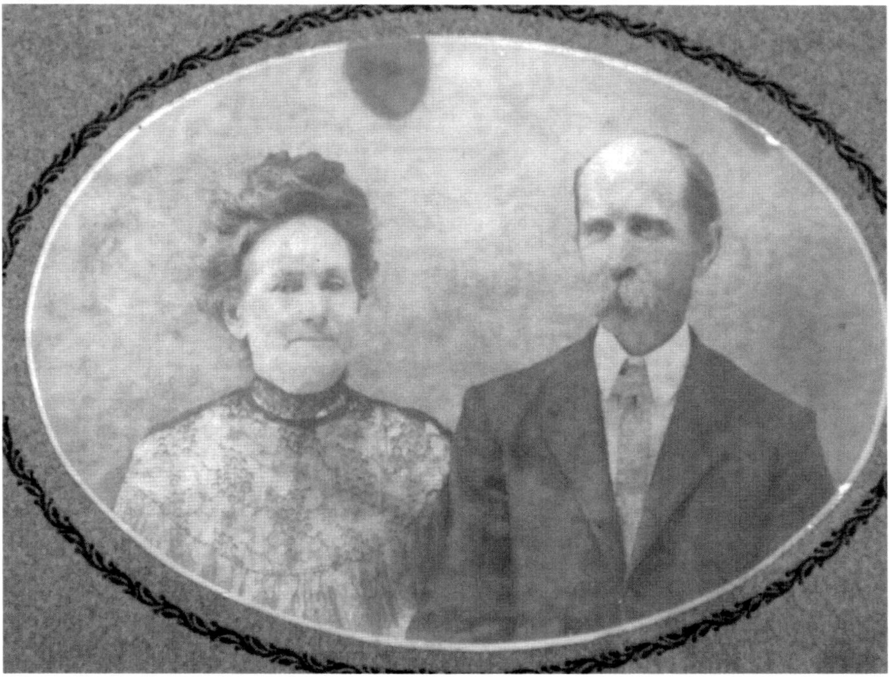

In 1874, David M. Simpson and his wife, Mary Vann Simpson, became the town's first settlers and were instrumental in setting the direction of the town. *Mount Dora Historical Society.*

confusion of Reconstruction, a flood of Yankee carpetbaggers fanned out across the conquered states, always ready and willing to exploit struggling southerners for personal gain. In Florida's Panhandle at the Jefferson County plantation of Milton Simpson, the war's end resulted in more than one hundred slaves being freed from his employ. While this was great news for them, it was bad news for Milton and his business.

By 1874, Milton's son, David, sensed that he would find better opportunities farther south. Like any headstrong twenty-two-year-old, he was not afraid to pursue his vision. He put his wife and children into a wagon and left Florida's rural Panhandle for the desolate heart of central Florida. Stopping in Mellonville (later Sanford), the story goes that Simpson took a break to join a friend on a hunting excursion. The two worked their way west from Mellonville, and about twenty miles later, they reached a crest on a hill above Lake Dora. Aside from a lone squatter on the land, all David could see was natural beauty, and far more importantly, he could see his future.

After purchasing 160 acres for just $300, David Simpson became the first homesteader. Excited about his purchase, he wrote to his father, described the

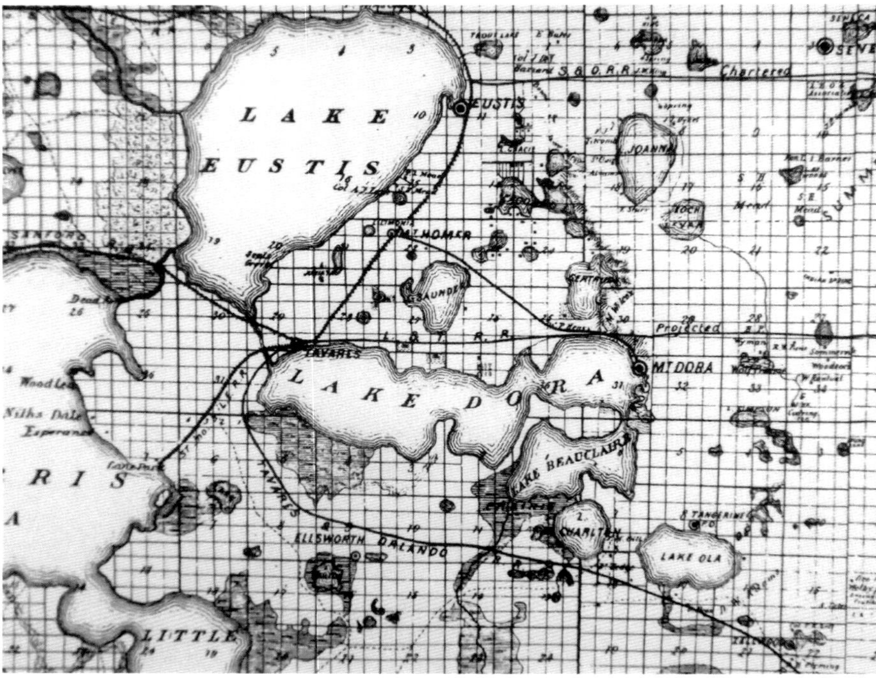

Lakes, railroads and some early settlements that wouldn't last highlight this map from the 1880s. Mount Dora, on the east end of Lake Dora, would survive. *Mount Dora Historical Society.*

landscape and encouraged him to come down and invest. By the following year, Milton had acquired 160 acres near his son, and the two soon owned 320 acres of central Florida land. For David, the move proved to be a perfect fit for his dreams, confidence, work ethic, personality and business sense. He planted orange groves, milled lumber and found that the land more than held its value as he began subdividing his property at a very healthy profit. After selling most of his land, David simply moved to a new home he built on his father's nearby 160-acre spread.

Notably, the biggest increase in the Simpson portfolio was their expanding family. In time, David and Mary would have ten children, including James Simpson, the first white child born in Mount Dora. James would later become involved in banking, citrus and the development of the town, while his brother Monroe, an active merchant, would became mayor and their younger brother David S. Simpson would later serve as Mount Dora's postmaster.

As one of the community's most influential couples, the Simpsons were essential in establishing the fledgling settlement as a place of permanence, and what they achieved encouraged others to bet on the future of Mount Dora.

Over the next decade, the area began to take root and gain a stronger foothold as settlers arrived by wagon, by rail and by steamboat (and sometimes using all three) in their efforts to start anew. Those who toughed out the journey were rewarded with land that was naturally suited for development. A wonderful pine forest surrounded the town, moss-draped oaks provided plenty of shade and cypress and palm trees lined the shore of the clean freshwater lake. Lake Dora was just one link in the Harris Chain that flowed to the Ocklawaha River, which connected to the St. Johns, which emptied into the Atlantic Ocean. By any measure, it was an altogether enchanting place to create a community.

David Simpson surely thought so, as would several other founding fathers, as well as a founding mother.

An Early Glimpse of Mount Dora

In 1886, A.H. Cook shared his opinion of Mount Dora:

My acquaintance with this surpassing locality dates back to a period when the settlement was too primitive to be adorned with a name. If there is another place in Florida occupying as pretty a site as Mount Dora, and like her as completely out of the woods, as it were, being five miles from the present base of supplies, and having no land agents or others making superhuman efforts to boom it along, which has made more substantial progress, I have not seen it.

There is no place I know of which offers better chances for investment of capital. The town is situated on an extensive plateau, and on the sides of a line of high hills gently sloping to the water's edge, extending one and half miles along the eastern shores of Lake Dora. The outlook from the hillside homes of the people and from nearly every part of the plateau, upon the waters and islands of Lake Dora and Lake Beauclair is incomparable.

One does not gaze upon a vast body of water, whose dull sameness becomes monotonous, but we have here a perfect panorama of woods and water, studded with isles of palm and beautiful hammocks, distributed in such a pleasing and picturesque fashion that an observer, from his elevated position, imagines he can see half a dozen lakes rather than two.

Mount Dora is a veritable paradise.

Chapter 4

FOUNDING FATHERS (AND MOTHER)

Mount Dora is a picture once seen never to be forgotten, and as I stand on the mount overlooking the lake, I say, Here let me live, this is the most lovely spot I have ever beheld.

–Dr. C.R. Gilbert, 1882

Alone in a Strange Country

The Simpsons weren't alone in realizing that there was something special about this land on the lake. Soon other residents saw a "most lovely spot" where an individual could put their stamp on the future by dreaming of a better world and then building it.

Such was the case of Clark and Helen McDonald, whose arrival in May 1875 would affect the course of Mount Dora. In part, their decision to relocate from Toledo, Ohio, was based on their daughter, Annie. She had wed at sixteen and had a child soon after, but her marriage was hanging by a thread. She had separated from her husband, William Stone, twice before, but her parents believed that the marriage would stand a better chance if their daughter and son-in-law came with them to Florida.

In some ways, it worked out even better than expected, since the McDonalds would enjoy what may have been the most astute deal (or the luckiest break) in Mount Dora history. While prospecting for land,

Clark McDonald and William Stone saw two lots marked as worthless swampland. They purchased both parcels and staked their claims at just eighty cents per acre. As it turned out, due to an error in Gould's survey, the parcel wasn't part of a swamp; it was, in fact, very valuable waterfront property (which likely didn't sit well with David Simpson, who thought that he owned that land). Nevertheless, the purchase established McDonald and Stone as the true owners of what would become part of Mount Dora's business district.

The McDonalds loved their new home. Annie loved her new home. As it turned out, William Stone didn't really love his new home. Or Mount Dora. Or Annie. In May 1877, Stone disappears from Mount Dora (and from history), leaving Annie behind. Two years after being deserted, Annie hired Tavares attorney Alexander St. Clair Abrams to file for a divorce. In the petition, Abrams described Annie's plight, revealing the tenor of the new settlement when he asserted that William Stone "left her in the woods of Orange County, in a strange country."

It was likely a relief for Annie when she was granted a divorce on August 5, 1879. No longer saddled with William, the attractive divorcée was free to flirt with a handsome twenty-nine-year-old bachelor who had just arrived from Pittsburgh.

Enter J.P. Donnelly

With his strong profile, thick mop of dark hair and abundant energy, everyone could tell that John Phillip Donnelly was a very determined young man. He demonstrated that by leaving his job at a Pittsburgh steel mill and making his way to Florida in 1879. His story, which he shared in a talk more than forty years later, recalled the day he first saw Mount Dora:

> *One morning in 1879 I started on foot on the other side of what is now Winter Park and landed at Rock Springs at sundown. On my journey the next day just before sundown I came over a hill on what is now Highland Street and the wonderful glorious Lake Dora burst upon my vision. The sight swept me off my feet. I stood on the spot and feasted my eyes on the lake for half an hour.*

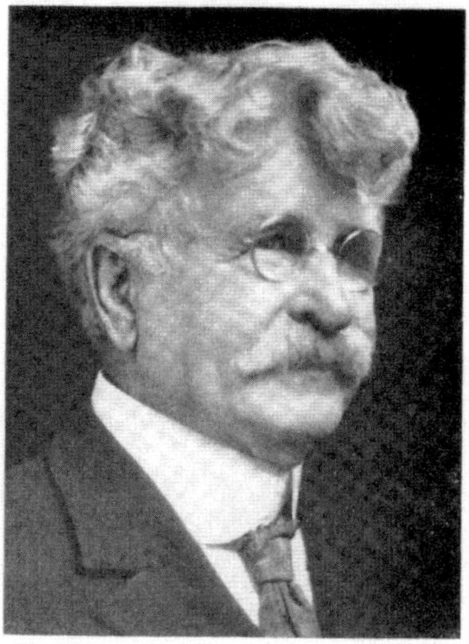

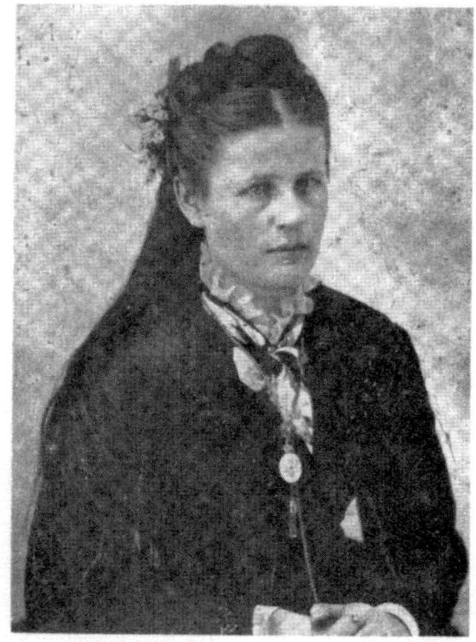

John and Annie Donnelly became Mount Dora's first power couple. *Mount Dora Historical Society.*

In this version (there were many others)*, he awakened himself from his trance and then walked on to Pendryville, where he could have put down roots had not the allure of Lake Dora lingered. Recognizing a better opportunity, Donnelly returned to Mount Dora and borrowed enough funds to invest in 160 acres of land. Lucky for him, his new neighbor happened to be the Widow Stone.

Over the next few years, a courtship developed. Donnelly had serious intentions for Annie and serious plans for their future. In July 1881, just two months after she and J.P. filed for their marriage license, Annie paid the balance (four dollars) on her ex-husband's homestead claim. As a result, she and her father owned an estimated two miles of Lake Dora waterfront. When J.P.'s property was added to the inventory, some of the most highly valuable parcels of real estate were now all in the family.

The couple was married on August 18, and it was clear from the start that Annie and J.P. would not only be husband and wife but business partners as well. At a time when women were not known for their independence or business savvy, Annie had it all.

**Donnelly was known for his tall tales. In an alternate version, he walked twenty miles from Winter Park, cut down trees to build a raft, paddled several miles across Lake Beauclair, was capsized by an alligator, subdued the alligator by shoving an oar in its mouth and then swam the rest of the way into Lake Dora, where he saw the town in the setting sun and thought, "This is for me."*

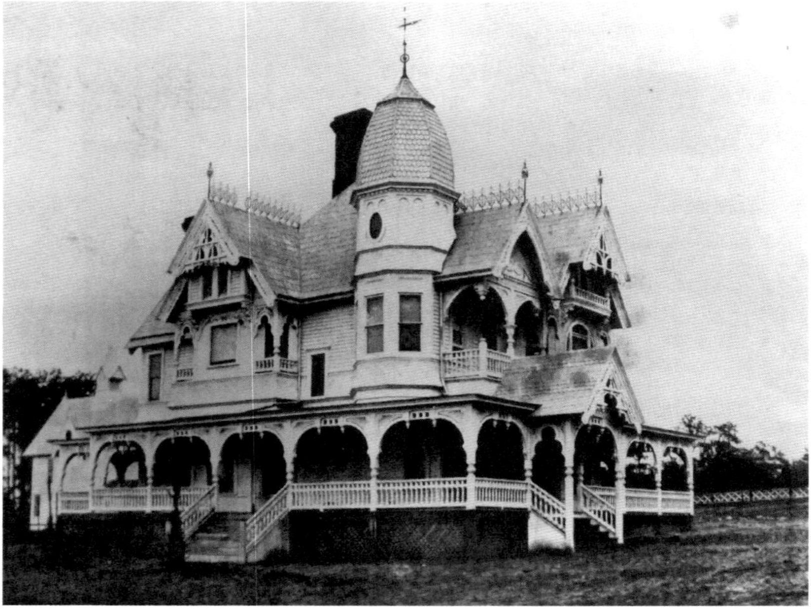

The combined fortunes of Annie and J.P. Donnelly are revealed in all their Gilded Age glory in the grand home the couple built in 1893. *Mount Dora Historical Society.*

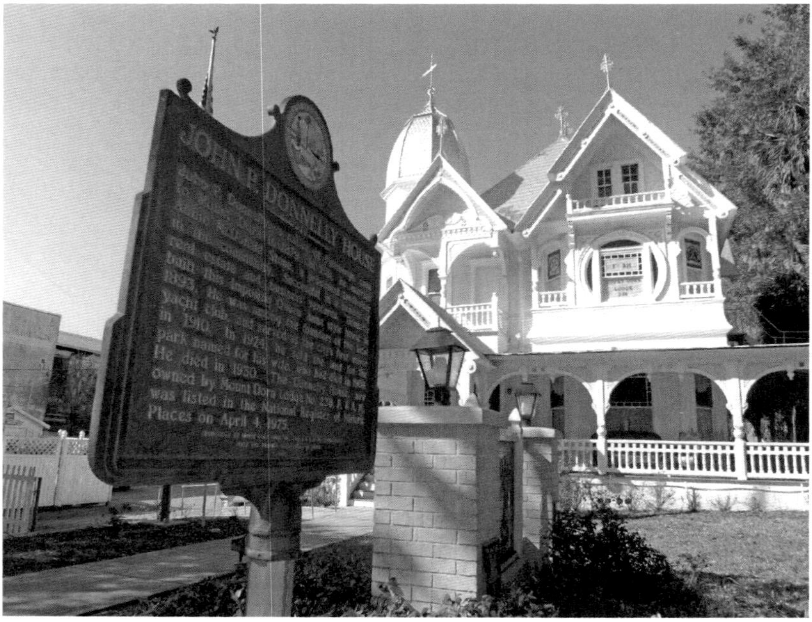

The 1893 Donnelly House was named to the National Register of Historic Places in 1975. It is now Mount Dora Lodge No. 238 of Free and Accepted Masons. *Nancy Howell.*

The newlyweds launched the most significant partnership in the town's history by reaching out to others to help develop the city. In 1883, they joined forces with fellow business leaders John Alexander and Eustis developer John MacDonald to build the Alexander House hotel, which would evolve into the Lakeside Inn. With a mixture of philanthropy and business acumen, J.P. and Annie would later donate lots for the Methodist and Congregational churches and contribute funds for the first fire brigade, as well as land for the cemetery. Indications of their impact on today's Mount Dora can be found in the naming of Donnelly Street and (Annie) Donnelly Park, as well as the 1893 Donnelly House, home of the Masonic Lodge, which has an ornate "Steamboat Gothic" style that makes it the town's focal point and most photographed icon in Mount Dora.

To be sure, it took more than the Simpsons, McDonalds and Donnellys to drive the town's direction. By the end of 1883, about fifty families lived in Mount Dora. Through their collective efforts, the settlement was taking shape.

A Few Founding Families

What the earliest settlers were creating began to generate buzz. Soon others were arriving from the Midwest, Mid-Atlantic and New England and helping set the course for the future. Among such influential families as the Bishops, Trues, Stowes, Powerses, Gateses, Brooms, Robies, Bruces and Rossiters were others, including the following.

The Tremains

Word about the community eventually reached Ross Tremain, who was living way up in Blue Earth, Minnesota. In 1878, he brought his family first to Eustis, and then in 1881, they relocated to a sixty-five-acre parcel purchased from—who else?—David Simpson.

The forty-year-old Tremain was inspired and energized by plans he had for the town. As a realtor, his fortunes improved as he sold his property to northerners two and a half acres at a time. Some of the proceeds were reinvested in Mount Dora's first packinghouse, a business that tied in perfectly with his role as grove supervisor for out-of-town growers. Tremain

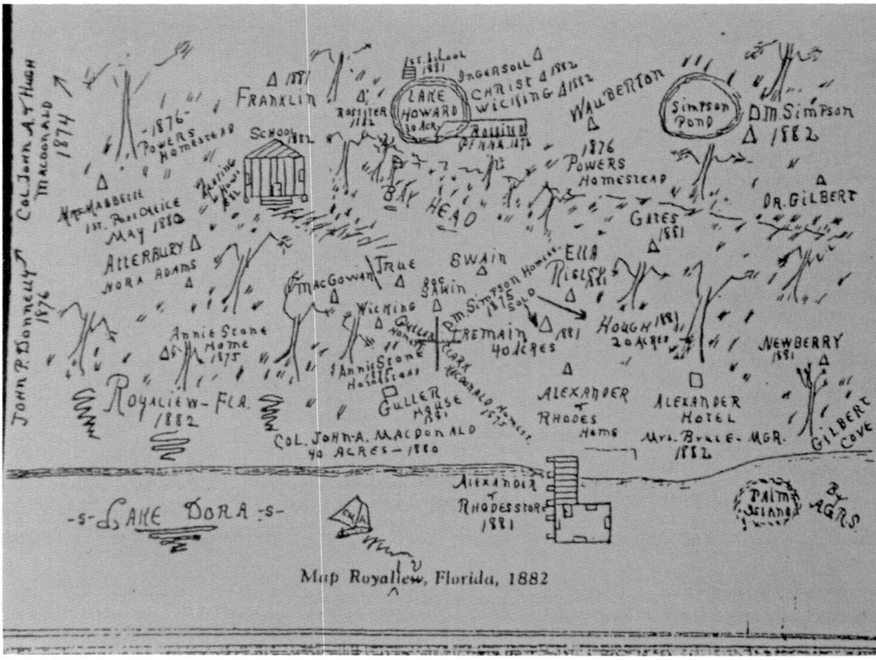

In the 1940s, Anna G. Rossiter Stowe, an early settler, wrote her memories of growing up in Mount Dora in the 1880s. She included a map showing the names and placement of homes and businesses. *Mount Dora Historical Society.*

and his wife, Georgia, also launched a Sunday school in their home, which led to the establishment of the Congregational church.

What's in a Name?

Considering that David Simpson was the first permanent resident of what would become Mount Dora, you may wonder why the town isn't named Simpsonville, Simpsonburg or Simpson City. After all, he was here six years before the Tremains arrived with their three children.

The answer is simple. After residents were successful in petitioning for a local post office in 1880, they soon realized "that place in the

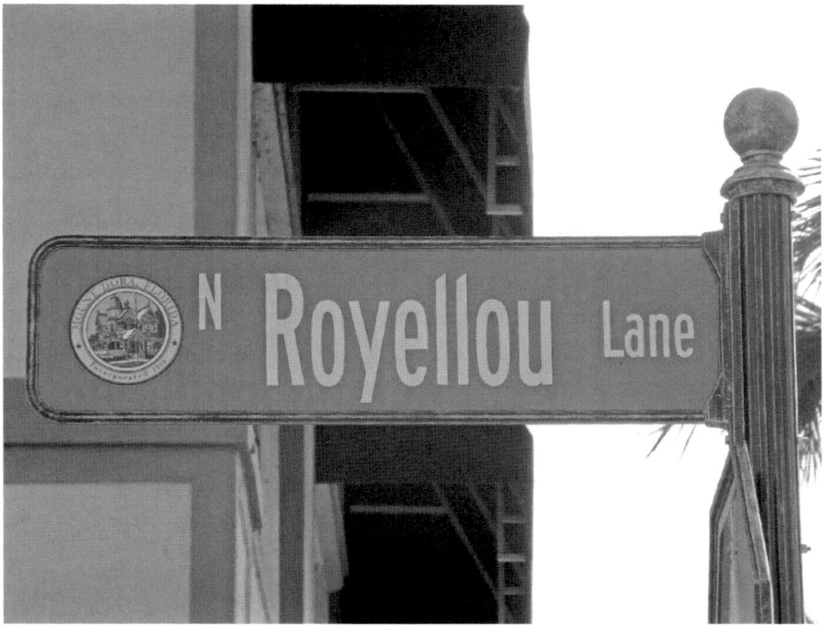

For one brief shining moment, Mount Dora was known as Royellou. *Nancy Howell.*

woods somewhere on the eastern shore of Lake Dora" would not fit on a postmark. Tremain—who later established himself as a citrus grower, college trustee and realtor—offered a better solution by suggesting the contraction "Royellou" from his children's names: Roy, Ella and Louis.

While the Tremain children must have been flattered to see their abbreviated names joined together on a postmark, their fame was fleeting. Not only was the name difficult to master and often misspelled (Royaliew, Royalview, Royallieu, Royallien, Royallen, Royallou, Royalune), there also seemed to be a disconnect between the name of the town and its most prominent feature, Lake Dora.

In late 1882, several residents decided to jettison the name, making its replacement an easy choice. Looking out at the calm, freshwater lake reflecting rolling hills that rose to a magnificent height of 184 feet above sea level, the name Mount Dora was proposed, seconded and then adopted on February 12, 1883.

The Alexanders

Retired colonel John Alexander and his wife, Ann, arrived from Kansas. John was given credit for suggesting the name Mount Dora as a replacement for Ross Tremain's preferred Royellou. Partnering with George Rhodes, Alexander opened a general store on the waterfront and later helped finance the construction of the Alexander House, which later became known as the Lakeside Inn. According to historian R.J. Longstreet, once the Pine Forest Cemetery was established, Alexander got a head start on the afterlife. He ordered his tombstone ("J.M. Alexander, Missionary"), and after it arrived, he loaded it into a wheelbarrow and rolled it to the cemetery.

The Sadlers

In 1884, Dr. Orin and Emma Sadler planted roots in Mount Dora. Then they planted orange trees. Following the Great Freeze of 1895, the Sadlers purchased and revived a three-hundred-acre grove in nearby Lake Ola. Emma Sadler, one of the most progressive and energetic women in town, would manage the groves whenever Dr. Sadler had to return to his native Pittsburgh for business. Not one to be idle, Emma also found time to promote Chautauqua and create the Mount Dora Improvement Society. Their son, Orin Jr., was an innovative lad—he strung a five-mile telephone line from his parents' grove to Mount Dora.

The Risleys

Encouraged to come to Mount Dora by his brother-in-law, Ross Tremain, Fred Risley and his wife, Nellie, arrived in 1882. Fred quickly established himself as a builder, contractor and operator of a cement plant. He popularized a textured concrete block ("Risley block") that can still be found in homes around Mount Dora. His influence reached well beyond the city limits, with hotels he built in Longwood, Sanford and Enterprise.

The Gilberts

Dr. Calvin Gilbert (who noted that Mount Dora was "the most lovely spot I have ever beheld") fought for the Union during the Civil War, after which he

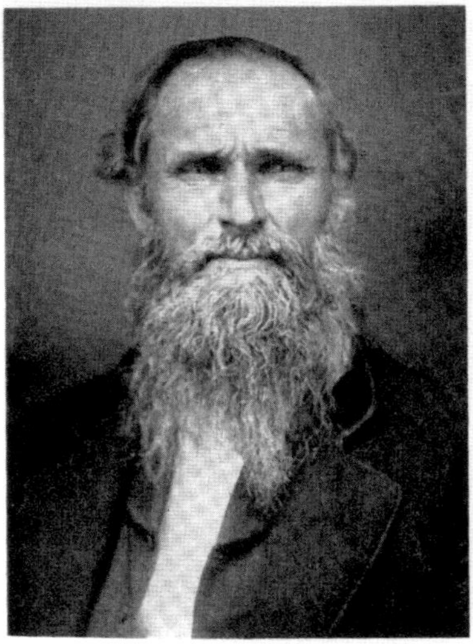

C.R. Gilbert, one of the first settlers, believed that Mount Dora was one of the loveliest places on earth—even after a freeze threatened his livelihood. *Mount Dora Historical Society.*

returned to his medical practice. Arriving in Mount Dora in 1882 with his wife, Margaret, and their five children, the family became active participants in the growth of the town. In addition to launching a citrus grove, Dr. Gilbert launched steamboats—the *Dispatch* and the *Dolphin*—which ferried passengers between Tangerine, Tavares and Mount Dora. Their son Earl Gilbert would provide land on reasonable terms for the town's African American residents. In 1922, Earl donated five acres of land by the shores of Lake Dora that became known as Gilbert Park.

The Edgertons

Charles Edgerton came from Philadelphia in 1895, a relatively late arrival by pioneer standards. But the move began a century of family involvement in the town, one that would have a direct impact on modern Mount Dora. In 1924, Charles joined other investors in the purchase of the Lakeside Inn, which would eventually be managed for more than forty years by his son Richard. Charles's other son, David, a realtor, also managed the Grandview Hotel and later captured images of the early days in his book *Memories of Mount Dora and Lake County.*

The Williamses

It wasn't only white settlers who were creating a community in Mount Dora. Living among them were former slaves and freedmen trying to scratch out a life in the wilderness. Among them were Nelson and Cynthia Williams. Nelson was the first child born to Isabella Williams, a slave who had been raped by her white master. As an adult, Nelson remained another man's property until he was freed at the end of the Civil War. First working at a turpentine mill in rural Island Pond, Florida, in 1879 he moved seventy-five miles north to Mount Dora. According to Dr. R. Eugene Burley in his book *Mount Dora: The Rest of the Story, Plus!*, Nelson and Cynthia settled in the town's northeast section and within a year had built a house and welcomed the first of seven children. By the 1880s, other families—among them the Butlers, Bowmans, Stricklands, Terringtons, Greens, Pages, Barneses and Codys—had joined the Williams family in what would become the predominately black district known as East Town. Other black settlers chose to be downtown, living in simple homes that stretched along Fourth Avenue from Baker Street to the shores of Lake Dora, where some lived on the picturesque waterfront.

Of Grave Concern: The Pine Forest Cemetery

The beginnings of the city's primary cemetery can be traced to J.P. and Annie Donnelly, who donated more than two acres on what was once the outskirts of town. For more than half a century, it was the Forest Cemetery until someone pointed out that nearly thirty other cities claimed a "Forest Cemetery." The "Pine" was added in 1953. Today, the burial ground covers about twenty acres situated between the Mount Dora Christian Academy and W.T. Bland Public Library. Tombstones help visitors deduce bits of the town's history, such as the tragedy of the Warburton family, whose four members drowned in 1882 when their wagon slid into Fiddler's Pond. There are also multigenerational family trees like those of the Aldermans, Butts, Dicksons, Donnellys, Fullers, Gilberts, Granthams, Hurlburts, Longstreets, Moons, Parkhursts, Peases, Rehbaums, Roseboroughs, Sadlers, Seabrooks, Shipes, Simpsons, Snells, Stokelys, Stutzmans, Tremains, Whites, Wileys and Wises.

www.uscemeteryproj.com/florida/lake/pineforest/pineforest.htm

Chapter 5

GET SMART

Two general stores, one drugstore, a carriage factory, three hotels, and two churches.
—J.P. Donnelly

SETTING UP CAMP

Compared to other developing central Florida communities, it was apparent that in the 1880s, Mount Dora was on the fast track. The town looked to the future with bold ideas and then worked to bring them to fruition. One of those ideas was Chautauqua, the traveling social and educational "camps" that brought a world of knowledge to primarily rural communities. Aware of the movement that was started in 1874 by Methodist bishop John H. Vincent, Mount Dora's city leaders began looking at ways to bring a Chautauqua to town.

Presented over the course of several days, speakers, performers, scholars, preachers and lecturers entertained audiences through comedy, music, speeches, sermons and theatricals, while educators shared lessons in literature, astronomy, history, science, art, architecture and theology. Chautauquas were a complete intellectual, religious and social experience—the pioneer equivalent of a TED talk and tent revival mixed together with Wikipedia and Woodstock.

By 1884, Chautauqua was spreading across America. From its base in upstate New York, it first found a footprint in Florida on the shores of Lake DeFuniak in the Panhandle town of DeFuniak Springs. As civic leaders began working

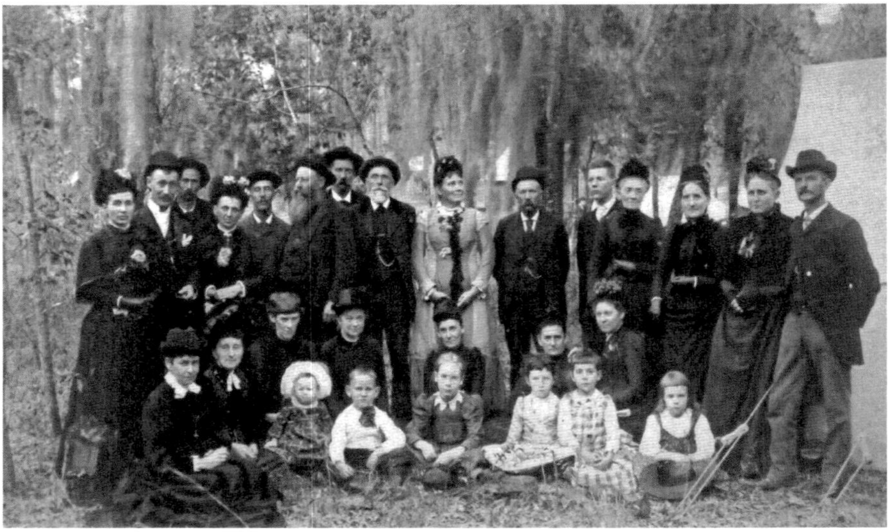

Happy campers. Attendees gather for intellectual, spiritual, recreational and social enrichment at the Chautauqua camp. *Mount Dora Historical Society.*

out the logistics to bring the event to Mount Dora, the first notice of the 1887 program appeared in the April 23, 1886 edition of the *Mount Dora Voice*. Offering a glimpse of the growing town and peek into its future, J.P. Donnelly pointed out that the community of 250 residents already enjoyed "two general stores, one drugstore, a carriage factory, three hotels, and two churches." Soon, he announced, they would be able to boast of a broad-gauge railroad and "the Congregational National Chautauqua Assembly."

Donnelly predicted that the camp would be visited by up to ten thousand attendees each winter. It's not difficult to imagine the effect this had on citizens who lived in a community barely a decade old. When Chautauquas were at their peak, families would travel for days to be entertained while being educated. The insights and discussions sparked by the experience likely inspired adults to explore new topics and, perhaps, encouraged younger participants to focus on a career.

In the Pines

As the big day approached, plans for the imminent arrival of Chautauquans started to fall into place. Arrangements were made for the Sanford train to make a stop in town en route to nearby Tavares. More importantly, organizers were able to secure a site for the gathering. Dr. W.P. Henry and his wife, Mary, generously donated a prime ten-acre parcel, an open area sprinkled with pines between lakes Dora and Gertrude—provided organizers furnished them with lifetime passes to the annual event.

Throughout the town and neighboring communities, flyers promoting the big event were being posted:

> *The grounds are beautifully located between Lakes Dora and Gertrude and on the Sanford and Eustis division of the Jacksonville-Tampa and Key West road. Two regular trains pass over this road each way—extra trains will be run if needed. Passengers, by either rail or boat, will be taken directly to the grounds. Excursion tickets at half rates. A dining hall and dormitory have been erected, and tents may be rented during the season.*

During its inaugural season of April 5–14, 1887, a giant tent was pitched to accommodate attendees who gathered to listen to a lecture on Japan, an address by the president of DeLand University and even a talk on "Love, Courtship and Marriage." Such was its success that by its sophomore year, in 1888, the new Hotel Chautauqua (two dollars per day, ten dollars per week) had been built to provide guests and visiting lecturers, writers, scholars and musicians with a place to socialize, rehearse and relax. But even four hotels weren't nearly enough to accommodate all the visitors seeking to enrich their lives, expand their horizons and enhance their social networks. Until more hotels could be built, guests had to look for lodging in the neighboring communities of Tangerine, Tavares and Eustis.

Part of the event's appeal were spectaculars featuring local luminaries, such as one of Mount Dora's earliest settlers, Mrs. Emma Sadler. As detailed by Harry Schaleman Jr. and Dewey Stowers Jr. in their article "Mount Dora, Florida—Chautauqua in the Wilderness," Sadler not only appeared as a speaker, but she was also an armchair producer. In 1895, she dazzled audiences with a staged presentation entitled "Sham Battle of the Blue and the Gray" in which local Civil War veterans from both sides of the conflict were back in uniform. Taking position in the woods beside the lake, veterans from surrounding communities reenacted a battle from what some locals called the War of Northern Aggression, replete with bugles, drums, blank ammunition and Rebel yells.

Chautauqua might have had an even larger impact on Mount Dora had it not been for the Great Freeze of 1895, which decreased the town's population and dampened its spirits. Then, following a 1905 fire that virtually

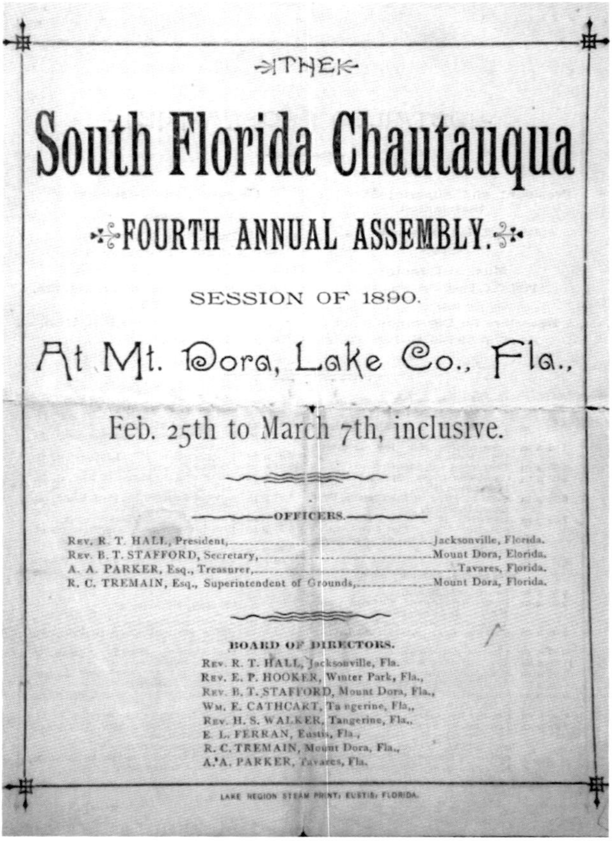

THE

South Florida Chautauqua

FOURTH ANNUAL ASSEMBLY.

SESSION OF 1890.

At Mt. Dora, Lake Co., Fla.,

Feb. 25th to March 7th, inclusive.

OFFICERS.

REV. R. T. HALL, President, ... Jacksonville, Florida.
REV. B. T. STAFFORD, Secretary, ... Mount Dora, Elorida.
A. A. PARKER, Esq., Treasurer, ... Tavares, Florida.
R. C. TREMAIN, Esq., Superintendent of Grounds, ... Mount Dora, Florida.

BOARD OF DIRECTORS.

REV. R. T. HALL, Jacksonville, Fla.
REV. E. P. HOOKER, Winter Park, Fla.,
REV. B. T. STAFFORD, Mount Dora, Fla.,
WM. E. CATHCART, Tangerine, Fla.,
REV. H. S. WALKER, Tangerine, Fla.,
E. L. FERRAN, Eustis, Fla.,
R. C. TREMAIN, Mount Dora, Fla.,
A. A. PARKER, Tavares, Fla.

LAKE REGION STEAM PRINT, EUSTIS, FLORIDA.

Left: The annual Chautauqua gatherings, which began in 1887, helped establish Mount Dora as a popular destination for out-of-state visitors. *Mount Dora Historical Society.*

Below: The Robert Burns Inn was one of Mount Dora's first hotels. It welcomed guests who arrived for the first Chautauqua of 1887. *Mount Dora Historical Society.*

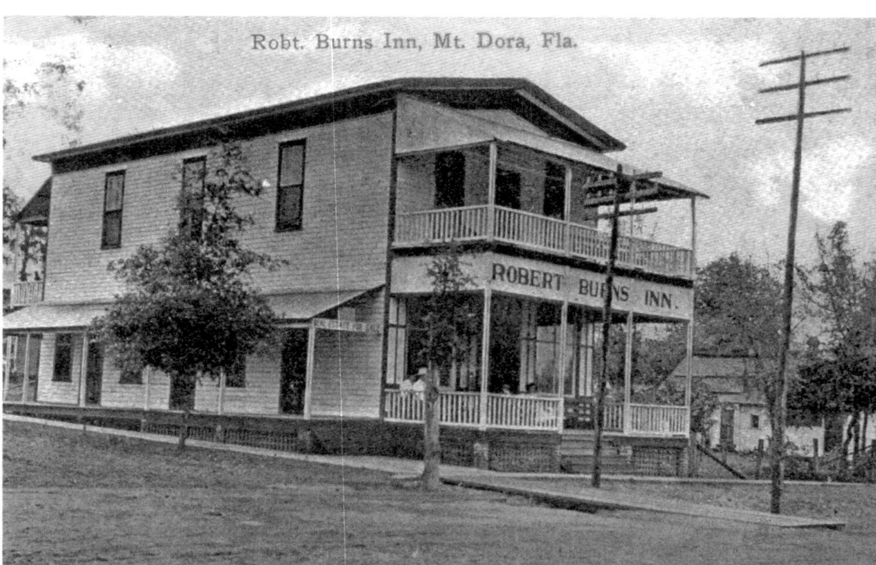

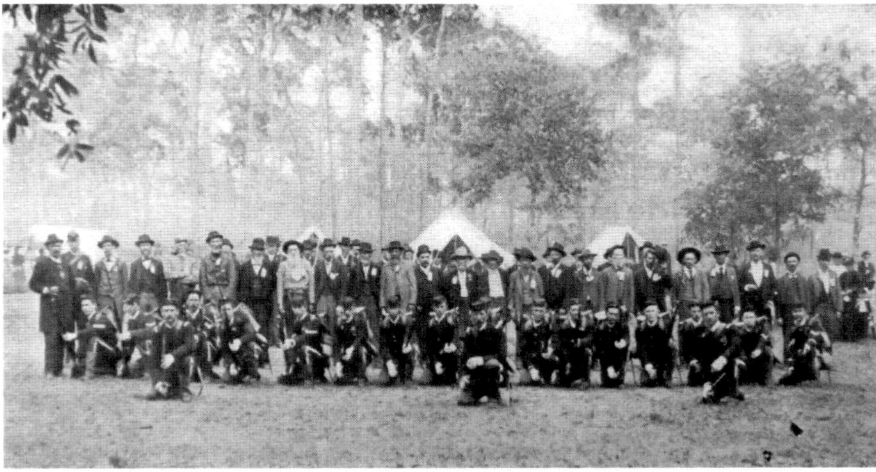

One last hurrah. In 1895, Civil War veterans and young reenactors gathered for a "Sham Battle of the Blue and the Gray" during the annual Chautauqua. *Mount Dora Historical Society.*

destroyed the camp along with the auditorium and hotel, the writing was on the wall. Regardless of its premature demise, the influence of Chautauqua most certainly helped set the town's direction. Before the fire extinguished what had been described as a "font of cultural greatness," Chautauqua showcased Mount Dora as a center for intellectual stimulation and social interaction—just as the Donnellys and Sadlers and Henrys had envisioned.

To this day, ripples of Chautauqua are seen in the diversity of Mount Dora's architecture, activities, events, festivals, visual and performing arts, religious denominations and even water sports and outdoor activities. With Chautauqua's heritage setting the way, the vision of the town founders continues to echo across Mount Dora and across time.

The Producer

No one knows how far the theatrical career of Mrs. Emma Sadler would have gone had frosts and fires not interfered with her well-received productions at the annual Chautauqua gatherings. Undeterred by the absence of Chautauqua, in 1904 Sadler found a new outlet for her talent and enthusiastic civic pride when she launched the Mount Dora Improvement Society.

Chapter 6

PICKING UP STEAM

A fine lot of coffins just received.
—Mount Dora Voice, *1886*

I Get Around

If any decade could be defined as Mount Dora's turning point, without a doubt it was the 1880s. By taking bold steps, Mount Dora avoided the fate of soon-to-be ghost towns like nearby Acron, Ethel, Chetwynd and Hawkinsville. Another factor elevating Mount Dora's status was its accessibility. While many travelers would still arrive by wagon or on horseback, not everyone had to rattle through snake-infested forests or hike on mosquito-infested trails to reach the town. Branching off the Ocklawaha River, a chain of lakes flowed from town to town, and visitors began to arrive via steamboats that puffed into a landing at Mount Dora's front door.

Ultimately, it didn't really matter whether a new resident arrived on foot, wagon, steamboat or train. If they had fought for the Union or Confederacy, or if they were dripping with wealth or just clinging to a dream, these early settlers seemed to possess the right stuff. Industrious and enterprising, they shared a similar work ethic, a common vision and a sense that somehow Mount Dora would give them an opportunity to reach their potential. Now it was their task to create a real town.

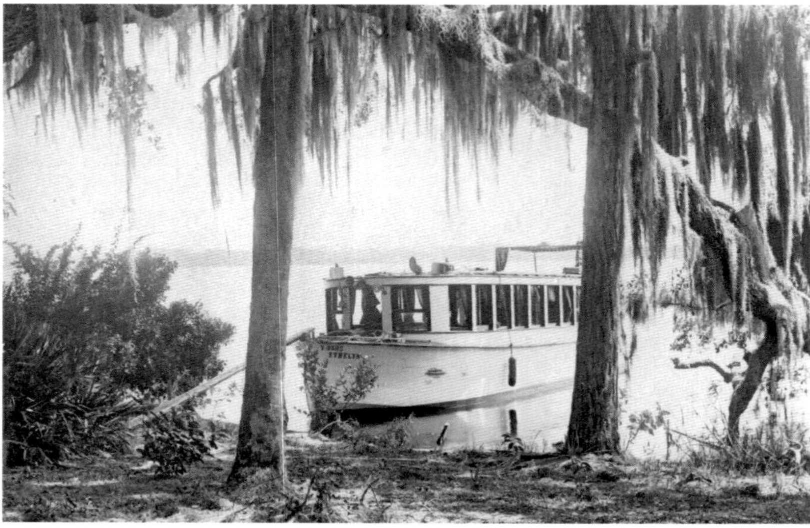

A day on the water was a popular pastime for boaters and anglers. Date unknown. *Mount Dora Historical Society.*

In addition to bringing new residents to the village, the chain of lakes was instrumental in expanding interaction with neighboring communities. In 1886, Dr. Gilbert bought an ad in the *Mount Dora Voice* to promote his water taxi service. For twenty-five cents, a passenger could board the steamer *Dispatch* en route to the town of Tangerine on Lake Beauclair. With Captain George Libby at the helm, the small craft would depart the wharf several times a day. Should a resident need to visit Tavares on the western end of Lake Dora, guests paid just fifty cents one-way or seventy-five cents for a round trip. To make a full day of it, for sixty cents Libby would ferry passengers from Tangerine to Tavares—a distance of roughly eight miles.

Getting Down to Business

If the town would have a future, it was agreed that one of the key projects would be the creation of a public school. Citizens petitioned the Orange County Board of Public Instruction, and on September 17, 1881, Public School District No. 59 was established. Land was donated, and a log cabin school was constructed near what is now Lake Franklin. At the head of the class was the town's first teacher: sixteen-year-old Edith Gates, daughter of settler Horatio Gates. The following year, the teenage teacher and her pupils moved into a comparably more modern school on the corner of Clayton Street and Seventh Avenue, where a potbellied stove kept them warm in the winter and where desks were fashioned from boards laid across blocks. When not in use by white students, the one-room schoolhouse was turned over, free of charge, to the trustees of "the colored school."

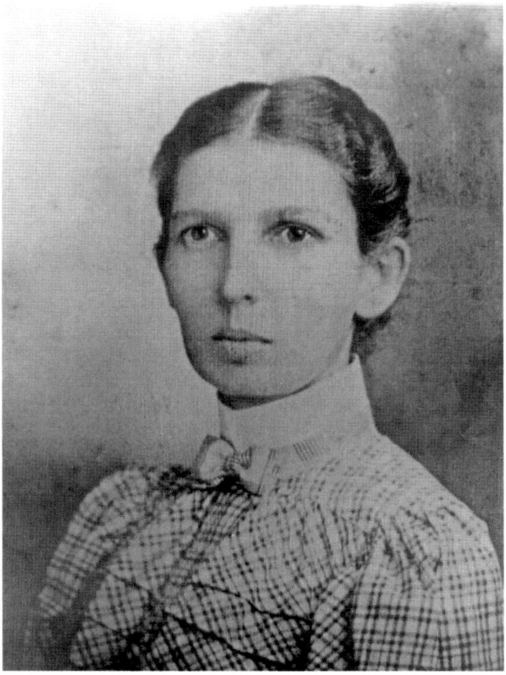

Edith Gates, daughter of settler Nathaniel Gates, became the town's first schoolteacher at the age of sixteen. *Mount Dora Historical Society.*

Another notable event came in 1886 when the *Mount Dora Voice* went to press. While the newspaper's run was brief (it barely lasted through the summer), it offered a peek at the evolution of Mount Dora. Only twelve years had passed since David Simpson built a log cabin here, and the newspaper's ads revealed that significant progress had been taking place. Much like today, real estate agents dominated downtown, and large ads reminded readers that land and lots were being sold by J.P. Donnelly, Colonel John Alexander, John MacDonald, Clark McDonald, A.F. Atterbury, W.G. Wright and Ross Tremain, who also served as a notary. Some the homes they sold had likely been designed by architect S.M. Sawin, painted by Charles Griffith and landscaped with plants selected from R.H. True's nursery.

All around town, services were available. You could stock up at Charles Stowe's general store, order a wagon from N.J. Kingman, pick up a harness for your horse from Albert Crossley and buy bushels of grain, hay and oats at Hill and Wyman's. Travelers had their choice of several new lodging establishments, including the Alexander House, the Bruce House, the Robert Burns Inn and the Guller House.

There was no cigar selection finer than that of Samuel X. Mullen (who likely had the town's *only* selection). There was a chair waiting for you at Joseph Sidney's tonsorial parlor (aka barbershop). Mrs. F. Sherman's drugstore had remedies for whatever ailed you, and if you felt very ill, you could visit Dr. W.C. Dodge. By the way, Hill and Wyman also sold hardware, and they wanted you to know that "a fine lot of coffins just received" (in the event you didn't reach Dr. Dodge in time).

Carving Out a County

The undercurrent of enterprise driving Mount Dora was also affecting many surrounding areas. The May 4, 1886 edition of the *Mount Dora Voice* carried a notice from the Orange County Board of Commissioners. It reported that voting Precinct 22 had been created from Tavares Precinct 18 and that registered voters were requested to add their names to the rolls prior to the next election—men only, of course.

Even more changes were on the horizon. Prodded by Alexander St. Clair Abrams of Tavares, on May 27, 1887, Florida's state legislature carved away 1,157 square miles of Orange and Sumter Counties to create Lake County. Mount Dora would now be on the new county's eastern border, six miles from the Lake County seat of Tavares and thirty miles from the Orange County seat of Orlando. To assess taxes in the new county, registrants were asked in 1888 to inventory and value their livestock. After tallying up all of the entries, F.B. Smith paid the most in taxes: $7.92.

By 1890, the census was reporting that 174 people (contradicting Donnelly's earlier estimate of 250) were living in the precinct of Mount Dora, which was slightly ahead of Higley's 161 but lagging well behind Altoona, a virtual metropolis with 463 residents.

From education to transportation, government to businesses, cultural to social endeavors, it seemed that nearly everything that could go right did go right for Mount Dora in the 1880s. Except for 1886.

Chapter 7

THE BIG CHILL

Another fearful day.

—C.H. Longstreet

Florida's Funeral

For many new residents who wagered their future on Mount Dora, the smart bet was a solar-powered industry: citrus. In the mid-1880s, an ad for Wright's Land Agency let readers know that *now* was the time to invest in a grove of your own: "The real estate men agree to send reliable information…from a lot in the pine woods worth $25 an acre up to a bearing orange grove worth $5,000 an acre."

Why shouldn't you invest? There were already seventy-five thousand orange trees growing within two miles of Mount Dora, the agency claimed, and you could get in on the ground floor. And with Mount Dora's temperate climate and good soil, planting an orange grove and picking profits from the branches seemed like a natural way to make a living. But Mother Nature had other ideas.

On Sunday, January 10, 1886, a severe freeze hammered Mount Dora. Green leaves turned black, branches cracked under the cold and thousands of oranges soon lay rotted on the ground. Pioneer C.H. Longstreet recapped in his diary the despair of residents: "The freeze came…we fear that everything is ruined. Dr. Gilbert has just been in saying 'This is Florida's funeral' and we all feel about the same way."

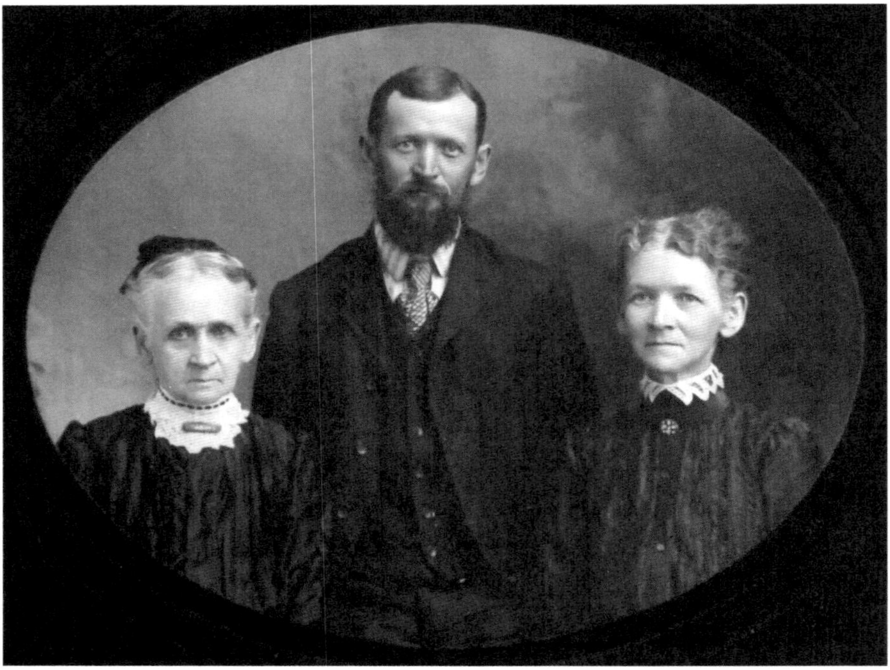

C.H. Longstreet, father of historian R.J. Longstreet, was filled with fear and anxiety during the Great Freeze of 1894–95. *Mount Dora Historical Society.*

During the week, the realization slowly sunk in: an entire industry and entire fortunes were being wiped out. Summarizing the collective mood of the community, Longstreet could scarcely work himself up to pen a few brief entries:

> *January 11: Another fearful day.*
> *January 12. This evening it actually snowed quite a little. Guess everything is ruined.*

Russell True, who had banked more than most in expectations of becoming a grower, wrote to his father in Ohio. He explained that in addition to losing all of his orange trees, he had lost pineapple, banana and guava plants along with 2,500 nursery trees and the potential income they would have generated.

As folks regrouped from the aftershocks of the freeze, they prepared for the future. Somewhere they had heard that the last arctic blast of this magnitude had swept through in 1835. So, in their thinking, this once-in-a-lifetime event was the worst nature could throw at them. Most assumed that a repeat of the rogue storm wouldn't come again for another half century.

They were off by about fifty years.

As Blue as Can Be

On Saturday, December 29, 1894, thermometers across the state were heading south. Temperatures plunged to fourteen degrees in Jacksonville, rose to a relatively balmy nineteen degrees in Ocala and dipped to seventeen degrees in Mount Dora. With his anxiety and anticipation escalating over the next few days, Longstreet returned to his diary:

> *December 28: Seems more like the freeze of '86 than anything we have had since.*
> *December 29: Every range was frozen solid and we think all of the trees are ruined. The disaster is overwhelming. Don't know how we will come out of it.*
> *December 30: No Sunday school. Too cold. Everyone feels about as blue as can be. One of our neighbors at sight of his ruined grove took a chill and went to bed sick.*

Bad as it may have seemed, there were some encouraging signs. Although the cold had killed many of the saplings planted after the Freeze of '86, growers saw that more mature citrus trees had survived and were actually sending out new buds. Most considered December's chill was the worst that could happen, but a cold north wind began to blow on Thursday, February 7, 1895. Slightly more than a month after "every range was frozen solid," temperatures plummeted yet again to an average of fifteen degrees. Throughout the long evening, residents could hear the sound of trees exploding like firecrackers as the sap inside froze solid. That single night killed many of the mature citrus trees that remained. The following day, Longstreet realized that Mother Nature was again at war with Florida. "An awful day," he wrote. "Worst that Florida has ever known…We are nearly ruined."

When the weather cleared, the damage was assessed. One news report told that a "universal scene of devastation overspread the orange-growing region of the state." In a letter dripping with sorrow, Longstreet shared the news with a cousin. He described the "magnitude of the calamity" and of the orange, lemon, grapefruit, lime, peach and guava trees that were dead and frozen to the ground, as well as the one-hundred-year-old cypress trees that also had been struck down by the wintry blast.

At the time, Florida's population hovered around 400,000. Following the statewide freeze, an estimated one-third of its residents packed up and moved out, leaving unfulfilled dreams frozen in the Sunshine State. "Many of our best people, who were in comfortable circumstances before the freeze are now really very poor," observed Longstreet. "Many have already left the state and many more are still going and more still would go if they could."

The freeze would trigger even more tragic events. Fred Risley's son, Carl, recalled the day when the owner of a successful citrus packinghouse in Paola (near Sanford) walked into what remained of his one-hundred-acre grove, surveyed the damage and then shot himself.

The Great Freeze of 1894–95 gave residents a hard, albeit necessary, lesson about life in Florida. While some gave up and moved on, those who remained in Mount Dora did so with the new knowledge they were at Mother Nature's mercy. Some adapted to the situation, switching to less costly and simpler crops like lettuce and cabbage. Others, like O.W. Sadler Sr. and James Simpson, decided to tempt fate. Wagering that the worst had happened, they purchased damaged groves at bargain prices, replanted and then waited. And then waited some more.

Citrus: The Sequel

Despite the financial and human toll of the Great Freeze, a combination of time, attention and more moderate winters would bring many of the groves back to life. One clear sign of the determination and tenacity of Mount Dora residents came in 1918 when the Mount Dora Citrus Growers Association was established. By learning lessons from successful growers in California, applying better agricultural techniques and keeping the groves warm during cold snaps, within fifteen years the cooperative managed by James Simpson could report it had returned $3.3 million back into the community through the workers and growers who had shipped more than 1.5 million boxes of citrus across the nation. Sweet success.

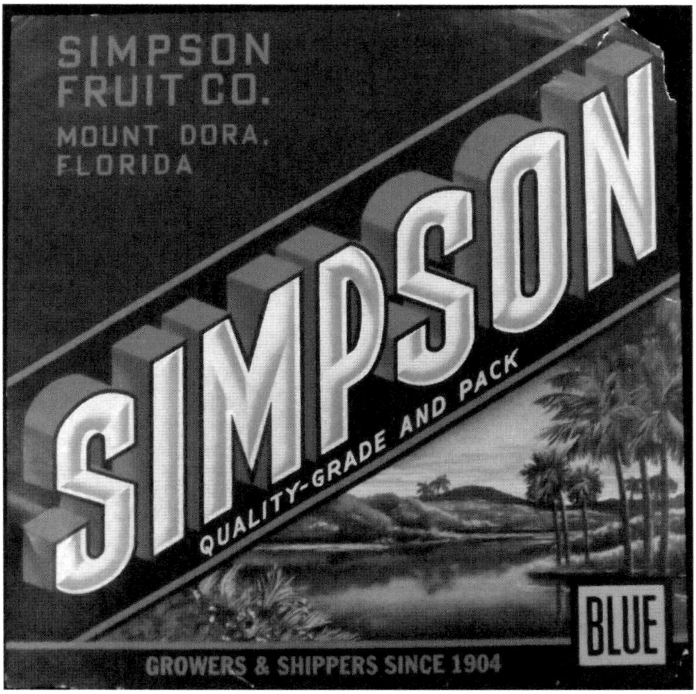

Even though others abandoned citrus following the Great Freeze, James Simpson was committed to the industry. The family still owns groves throughout the town. *Mount Dora Historical Society.*

Freeze Out

More than half a century after the Great Freeze of 1894–95, Lottie Clifford Taylor described the exodus from Mount Dora and the surrounding areas. It wasn't just citrus that had been affected, but also farms and groves filled with peaches, tomatoes, watermelons, vegetables and other sources of food that threatened to starve people. Add to that the loss of feed that also endangered the lives of horses, pigs and cattle and soon families were departing in droves, often leaving dishes on their dining tables and possessions behind. "Many people gave up, abandoned their homes, and moved away," Taylor recalled. "With no money, no work, and not much business, this was a paralyzed region."

Chapter 8

GETTING IN SHAPE

Now for streetlights, good roads, and the up-to-datest town in the State.
—Mount Dora News, *1910*

Talk of the Town

Freezes had crippled the citrus industry and a blaze had fizzled Chautauqua's future, forcing residents to look at different ways to turn a new settlement into a thriving town. To no one's surprise, they were up to the challenge. At the turn of the twentieth century, technology would help Mount Dora find its way.

Young Orin Sadler Jr., the son of pioneers Orin and Emma, was one of the first to recognize how telecommunications could improve commerce. Working from the concept that it would be easier to *call* Mount Dora rather than drive five miles from his family's Lake Ola orange grove just to deliver a message, in 1900 he loaded up his buckboard wagon with a ladder, two hundred porcelain knobs and several spools of telephone wire and headed out. With a helping hand from Thomas Washington, an African American who worked with the Sadlers, and David S. Simpson, who was dating (and would later marry) Orin's sister, Josephine, the three friends climbed pines, poles and fence posts until they had tacked up five miles of wire between Sadler's grove in Lake Ola and a switchboard installed in Monroe Simpson's downtown Mount Dora store. The buzz this generated prompted other businesses and residences to get in on the action. So, once again, young Sadler and his pals shinnied up trees and poles until about three dozen customers were connected. Without realizing it, Sadler, Simpson and Washington had created the town's first modern communications network.

In early 1910, the town's infrastructure was about to get another boost. A notice in the *Mount Dora News* (the town's first newspaper since the *Mount Dora Voice* folded in 1886) encouraged citizens to attend a town hall meeting on March 25 for "the purpose of electing officers and incorporating the town of Mount Dora."

On that Friday evening, James Simpson, son of the town's first settler, grabbed a handful of letterhead stationery from his citrus packinghouse and hurried to the meeting. About forty of the town's leaders gathered to discuss and debate Mount Dora's future as James scribbled the minutes. When it was time to vote, Simpson took note and announced the results. With thirty-nine ballots cast, thirty-one were for incorporation and eight were opposed. The majority decision would shape Mount Dora's future, making it easier to organize the town's development, collect taxes and reinvest in growth.

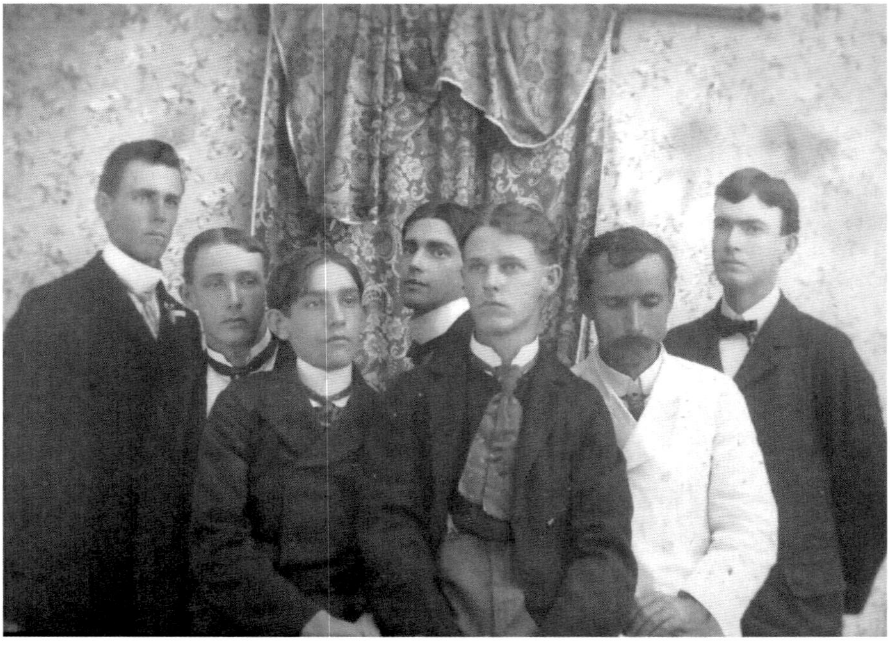

The Methodist-Episcopal Sunday school class of 1900 included several future town leaders. *Left to right*: James Simpson, Claude Vrooman, Sam Sadler, Orin Sadler Jr., Lloyd Vrooman, Earl Gilbert and George Butler. Orin and James's brother, David, would string the first telephone lines, and Earl would contribute a city park. *Mount Dora Historical Society.*

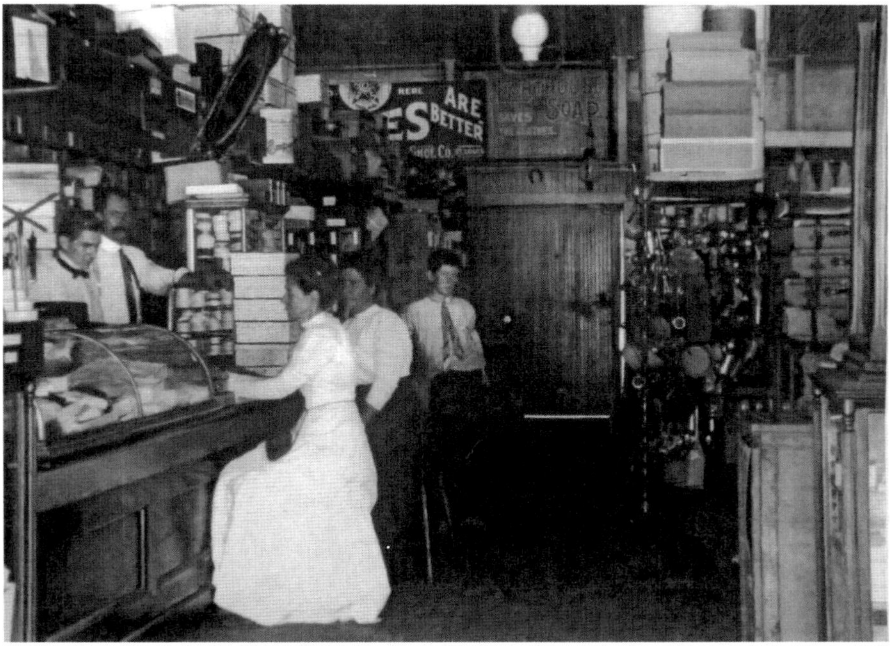

Son of town founders David and Mary Simpson, Monroe V. Simpson (*behind counter*) ran a general store and, later, became the town's mayor. *Mount Dora Historical Society.*

The *Mount Dora News* reported:

> *The galleries of the Town Hall were filled with spectators, mostly ladies who were very much interested in the outcome of the election and who showed their appreciation of the result by an ovation to the newly elected officers which they never will forget.*

Following the unforgettable ovation, it was time to celebrate:

> *After the election was over the crowd assembled at the drugstore where the boys had to "set 'em up" good and hard. They then adjourned to the residence of the newly elected mayor and didn't go home 'til morning.*

The Driving Force

The new government, consisting of Mayor J.P. Donnelly and seven aldermen, was now in place and facing a series of tasks. Mount Dora needed paved streets, streetlights and sidewalks. At the time, the town didn't have a police department, a fire department or any water systems. What it had was a wellspring of enthusiasm and support, particularly from the *Mount Dora News*, which heralded the major changes to come, such as "streetlights, good roads, and the up-to-datest town in the State."

To achieve this, the city council got down to business. In one of their first meetings, council members voted to buy eight streetlights to be placed around the town. Over the next several months, they made plans and tracked their financial progress. They were pleased when treasurer E.C. Stovall reported that $74.20 had been collected in taxes. The following month, Stovall collected fees for dog licenses that increased the town coffers by $3.00.

Council members were getting a feel for operating an efficient government. They agreed to purchase a half dozen street signs and then voted to "straw the roads." Cheaper than paving (an option the city couldn't afford anyway), "strawing" involved laying a bed of straw over dirt or clay or mud to make the roads navigable for carriages as well as the handful of automobiles that passed through town. Bidding the job at a modest sixty dollars per mile, Jeff Franklin won the contract.

By the close of 1911, city taxes had generated nearly $900. Two years later, the town marshal was given the authority and a budget of $110 to build a jail. He was also granted permission to buy a badge and a pair of handcuffs.*

By most accounts, it appears that good roads were the primary focus of the council. By mid-1913, it had approved a $12,000 bond to pave a few heavily trafficked roads, although months later it also approved another "strawing of the roads," which was welcome news for Jeff Franklin, who again won the contract. But in the summer of 1914, councilman James Simpson was sent to Cape Cod on a mission to inspect its "oil sand roads." Three weeks later, Simpson reported that these were just the sort of roads that Mount Dora deserved. At just sixty-five cents per square yard, it was a bargain. Better roads meant that more drivers could now zip through town, but at no more than fifteen miles per hour, since the council had passed that law as well.

With the incorporation of the city, the floodgates of progress had been opened. Now the pace was about to pick up.

**The marshal's handcuffs would come in handy in the event he saw a cow out for a stroll. Responding to citizens who complained about the rattling, echoing sound of their bells, the council passed an ordinance making downtown off-limits to cows after dark. No more cowbell!*

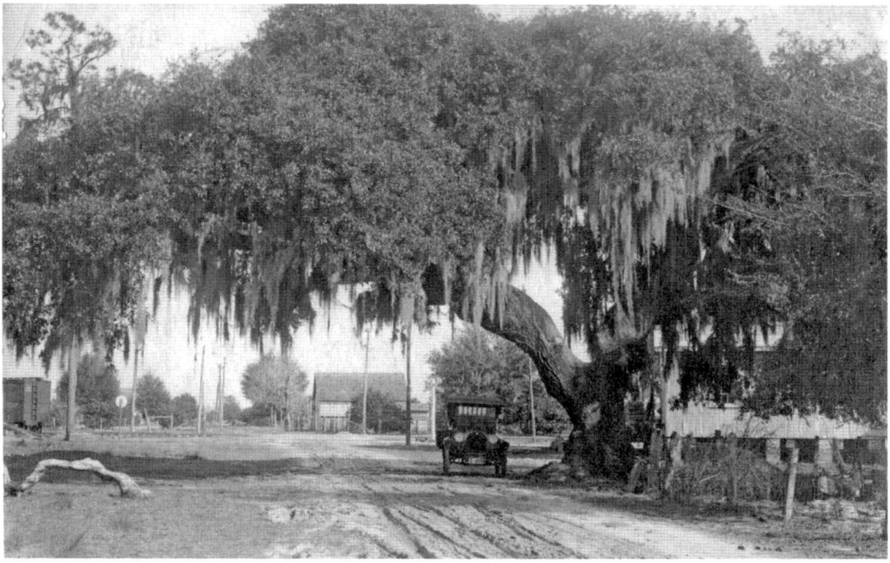

Out for a drive on yet-to-be-paved roads reveals Mount Dora's rural nature nearly a century ago. *Mount Dora Historical Society.*

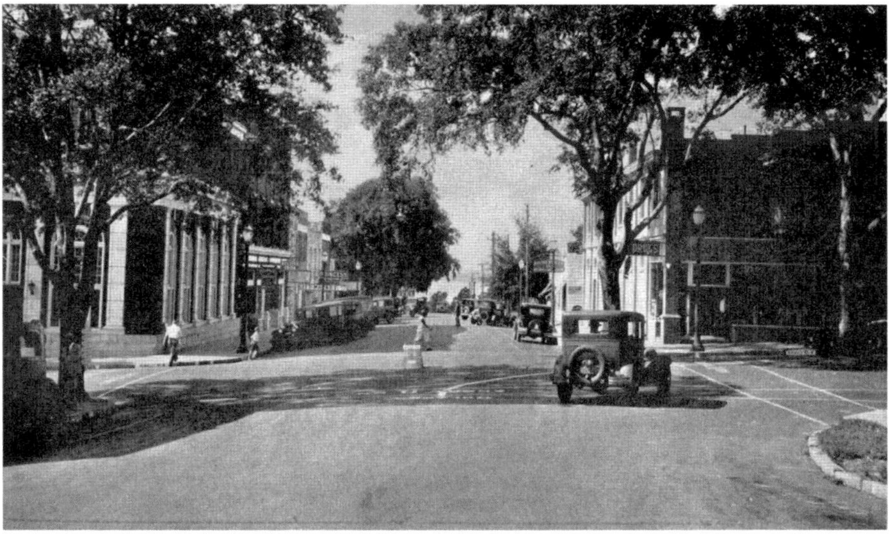

By the 1920s, paved roads and concrete sidewalks were creating a modern town. In this scene, the intersection of Fifth Avenue and Donnelly Street was, and remains, the epicenter of the business district. *Mount Dora Historical Society.*

Flashback to 1913: Clear Sailing

On the west end of Fourth Avenue overlooking Lake Dora sits the Mount Dora Yacht Club, the oldest inland waterway yacht club in Florida.

According to historian Martha Herron, its history began in May 1913, when Henry C. Fuller and fellow boat owners acknowledged their shared interest of boating, formed the club and drew up articles of incorporation. Lakefront land was purchased from Charles and Cora Fuller, and $5,000 was invested in building a new clubhouse. That October, members celebrated the opening of the new clubhouse, while locals closed their businesses and headed to the shore to witness the first regatta showcasing powerboats racing across the water. Little could dim their passion for these highly anticipated, thrilling, high-octane races—at least until World War II.

At the war's inception, many club members reported for duty, and regattas were scuttled when gasoline was rationed. Remaining members helped the war effort by assisting the Coast Guard in patrolling Lake Harris and by keeping the club open to serve as a USO center. During the war, an estimated seventeen thousand service men and women were welcomed and entertained at the club. In the 1950s, sailboats replaced powerboats at the annual regatta, and the club began offering sailing lessons to young students. The original clubhouse was lost to a fire in 1966 and replaced by the current clubhouse, which features beautiful views of Lake Dora, a dining hall, a dance floor and a bar area.

Considered the social center of Mount Dora in the early days, the yacht club continues its socials and hosts the annual Sailing Regatta every March.

www.mountdorayachtclub.com

Chapter 9

THE ROARING '20s

No "ifs" or "ands" about it. Mount Dora is to become one of Florida's most important inland cities.

—Mount Dora Topic, *1924*

People-Powered

By the 1920s, there were new roads, new streetlights, new businesses and an assortment of new social and civic clubs. Community leaders and entrepreneurs could see unlimited possibilities for Mount Dora. As a result, a group of businessmen headed by Robert N. "Bob" White formed the Mount Dora Development Club. To demonstrate their faith in the city's future, the seven charter members agreed to launch a miniature real estate boom whereby each one committed to building a single-family home.

As a means to gain support of local residents, White then suggested a partner organization, the Mount Dora Commercial Club, which would later evolve into the chamber of commerce. With the public-oriented Commercial Club largely supporting the business goals of the Development Club, the process began to take shape. Another beneficiary of this partnership was the city council, which was open to discuss, refine and approve a variety of citizen-initiated ideas that led to more buildings, an ice plant, waterworks, expanded paved roads, fire protection and attractive new neighborhoods and subdivisions.

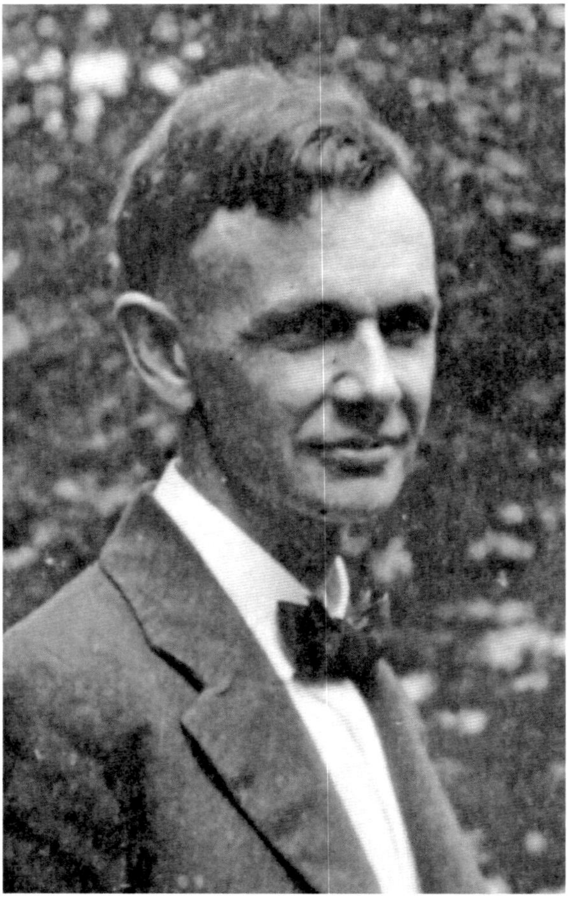

Left: Robert N. "Bob" White was one of the town's most active promoters, launching the Mount Dora Development Club and the Mount Dora Commercial Club, which became the chamber of commerce. *Mount Dora Historical Society.*

Below: Composed of the town's civic leaders, members of the Noonday Club (later the Kiwanis Club) meet in 1921. *Mount Dora Historical Society.*

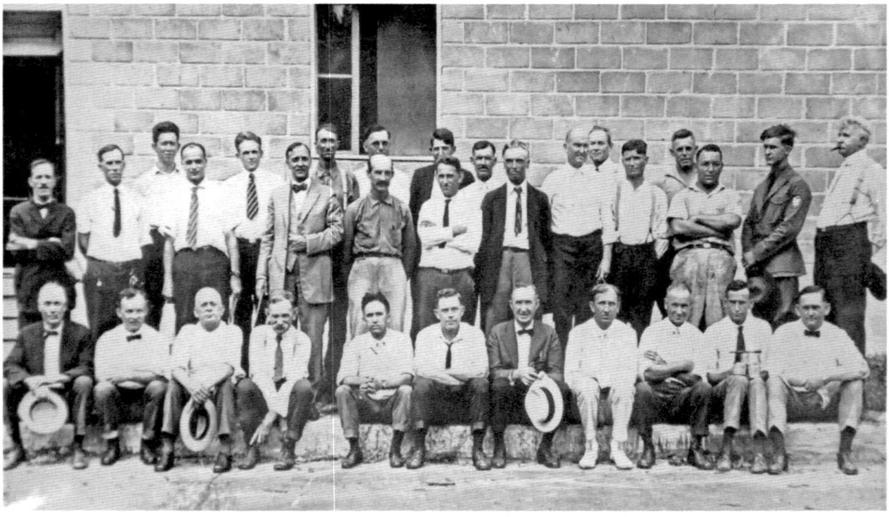

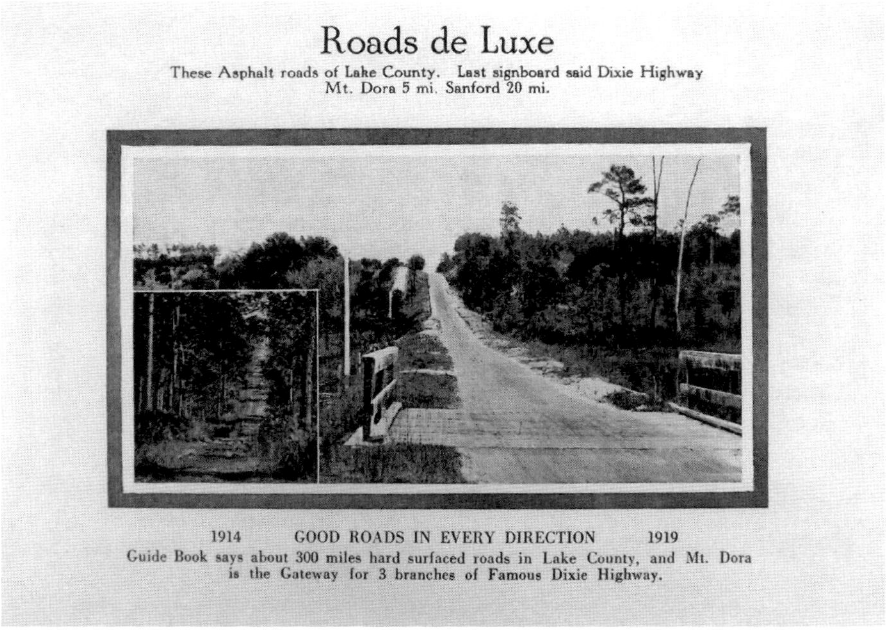

Hoping to entice tourists as well as potential residents, promotional pamphlets celebrating paved roads and other aspects of Mount Dora living were widely distributed in the 1910s and 1920s. *Mount Dora Historical Society.*

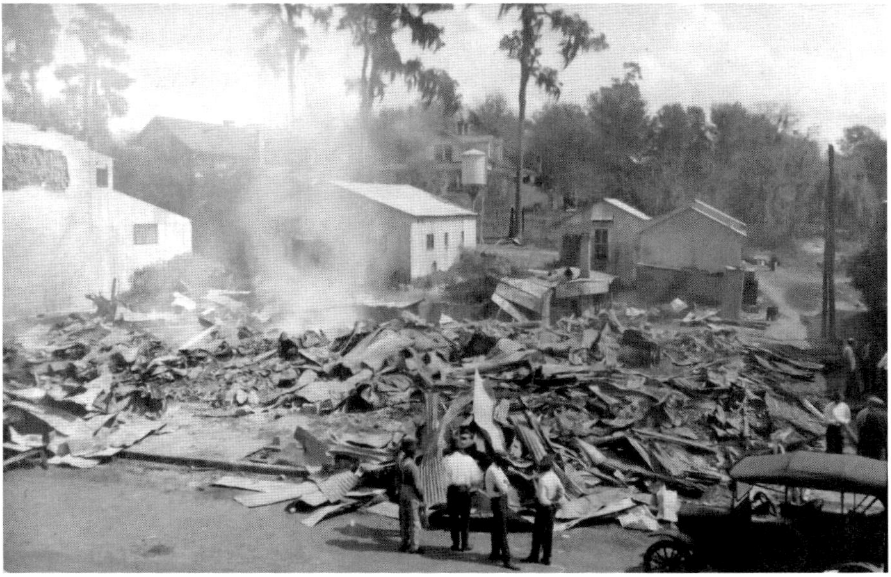

A 1922 fire still smolders after burning down much of the east side of Donnelly Street in the heart of town—a temporary setback amid overall prosperity. *Mount Dora Historical Society.*

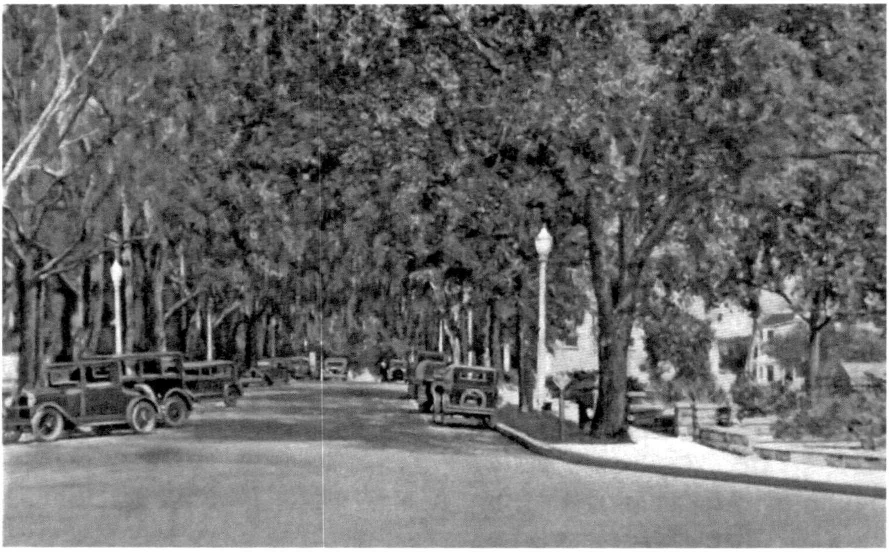

This postcard from the 1920s enticed tourists with Mount Dora's paved streets, streetlights, a canopy of oaks and always warm and sunny weather. *Mount Dora Historical Society.*

With this public-private alliance in place, members of the Commercial Club agreed that they needed to bring more travelers to Mount Dora. To accomplish this, White went out and photographed ordinary scenes around town—quaint houses and gardens, the downtown district, recreational activities, the beautiful lake and setting sun—and then he created a promotional booklet. To make sure that people knew how to reach this picturesque community, the grass-roots publicity campaign included promotional signs posted between Mount Dora and Washington, D.C. Impressed by the club's initiative to lure tourists, the city council voted to compensate it $260.96 toward its advertising costs.

In anticipation of the arrival of new visitors and potential permanent residents, the town continued taking major steps toward modernization. A property assessment was earmarked for additional paved streets and new curbs, nearly $50,000 went toward the purchase of electric light facilities installed by the Eustis Light & Water Company and $90,000 was invested in a city sewage system. At the same time, one could witness the wide arc of the council's role. Not only was it tackling big ideas, but at an April 1923, council meeting officials also took up the pressing issue of free-range chickens. After some debate, it was decided that chickens could not roam free within city limits. Meanwhile, Bob White's friendship with a wealthy visionary would lead to some big changes in Mount Dora.

On the Waterfront: The Story of Boathouse Row

Contributed by Jane Trimble

Although Mount Dora has changed far beyond the imagination of its original settlers, there has been one constant. Ever since Clark McDonald managed to secure nearly two miles of waterfront in the 1880s, there has been a common desire to live as close as possible to the waters of Lake Dora. You can't get any closer than Boathouse Row. Writer and historian Jane Trimble researched the origins of these quirky and unique waterfront residences.

An intriguing part of Mount Dora's lakefront, Boathouse Row's exact origin is ambiguous: It was a fish camp. It was built for commercial purposes. It was because a wooden boat works was located there. These are some of the answers longtime Mount Dora residents provide about the history of Boathouse Row, a small stretch of eclectic homes perched on pilings on Lake Dora's eastern edge. However, the definitive answer—backed up with historical facts—to why and when Boathouse Row began was elusive.

The earliest dated information uncovered was a vintage colorized postcard with the caption, "Boat House Row/Mount Dora, FL—1907." The postcard shows three boathouses on the eastern shoreline of Lake Dora with boats out on the water. Reference librarian Greg Phillips located a 1921 land survey of the property belonging to a Mr.

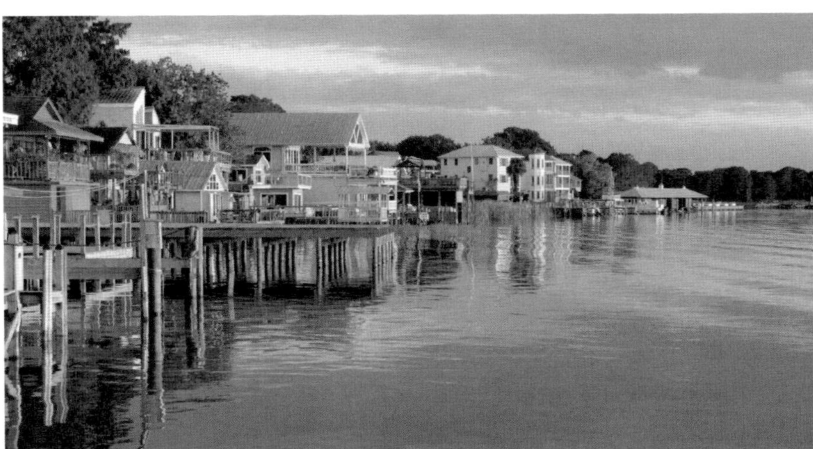

In the 1920s and 1930s, Boathouse Row really *was* a row of boathouses. Today, they have been converted into wonderful waterfront homes. *Steve Williams.*

White indicating there were twelve boathouses built when the lake was part of the transportation system for the citrus industry.

Often mentioned in Boathouse Row history is Wise Boat Works. Mount Dora native Edee Waite Robinson shared an excerpt from Eldon and Martha Herron's *The Mount Dora Yacht Club Commemorative History 1913 to 1993*, in which the owner of the Minnesota boat building company, Harry Wise, was commissioned to build a wooden sailboat for the yacht club in 1921. Some members also commissioned Wise to build boats, including Charles Edgerton, president of Lakeside Inn.

Edgerton was impressed with Wise Boat Works and determined it should move to Mount Dora, which it did in 1926. Edgerton bought a boathouse on Boathouse Row and financed the business, and Wise Boat Works operated for a number of years. The boathouse still remains at the end of Boathouse Row. Next to it stands a metal container for the wood chips and sawdust—the byproduct of wooden boat construction.

The 1940s and '50s ushered in the remodeling period of the boathouses. Tired of driving back and forth for weekend fishing excursions, some of the owners began renovating their simple boathouses, with apartments and more elaborate homes being built atop the original pilings.

Boathouse Row remains one of the more unusual and intriguing neighborhoods in Mount Dora, with homes that now range from rustic to ritzy. And while neighbors may be stacked too closely together and it can be a challenge to access via a single lane, the twenty-some residents of Boathouse Row feel they have found paradise. An historic sanctuary that comes with peace, tranquility, quiet…and a 4,475-acre backyard called Lake Dora.

A Shore Thing

One of the most influential investors to arrive in Mount Dora was Lewis R. Heim. His fortune had been made with such inventions as the "Picker-Roll for Hatting and Fur-Refining Machinery" and the "Heim Centerless

Cylindrical Roll Grinder" for manufacturing ball bearings. Heim first came to Mount Dora at the invitation of his friend Bob White, who had been his student at a Connecticut Sunday school. Impressed by White's unbridled enthusiasm for Mount Dora, Heim's interest was piqued. He felt certain that there was *something* worthwhile going on here. When he returned to Mount Dora in 1924, it was without the benefit of his friend Bob, who passed away at the age of thirty-eight in April 1923. Despite this, Heim's enthusiasm grew even more when he met real estate salesman George Malone.

By all accounts, Malone was good at his job, and he proved this by selling lots on the old Chautauqua site. Even though the land on Lake Gertrude had become an overgrown jungle following the fire that torched the 1,500-seat auditorium and hotel nearly twenty years earlier, it didn't seem to faze Malone. More importantly, it didn't seem to faze Heim, who had bigger visions for the land.

After purchasing hundreds of acres, Heim, the new owner and developer, launched the first of three full-scale clearings to prepare the grounds for major development. Next he enlisted Orin Sadler Jr. to survey the development. As an enticement to buyers and future residents, Heim started a promotion that promised a free lot to anyone who could name the subdivision. When Lavonne Lashar's suggestion of "Sylvan Shores" won the contest, she won the lot.

Now it was full speed ahead. Choosing to keep Sylvan Shores separate from the city, Heim proceeded to bankroll nine miles of streets and sidewalks, water mains, streetlights and actual telephone lines. He was also prepared to help homeowners finance their new homes. To promote the budding community, Heim also approved weekly full-page ads that Malone prepared.

A Gift from the Gilberts

Among the first philanthropists to give back to the city was Earl Gilbert, son of one of Mount Dora's first settlers. In 1922, he contributed five acres of land at the east end of Lake Dora, and the city acknowledged his generous gift by naming it Gilbert Park. Today, the park features a playground, picnic pavilions, barbecue grills and a flowing creek named in honor of former mayor Paulette Alexander. With views of beautiful sunsets, Gilbert Park remains one of the city's most active public spaces.

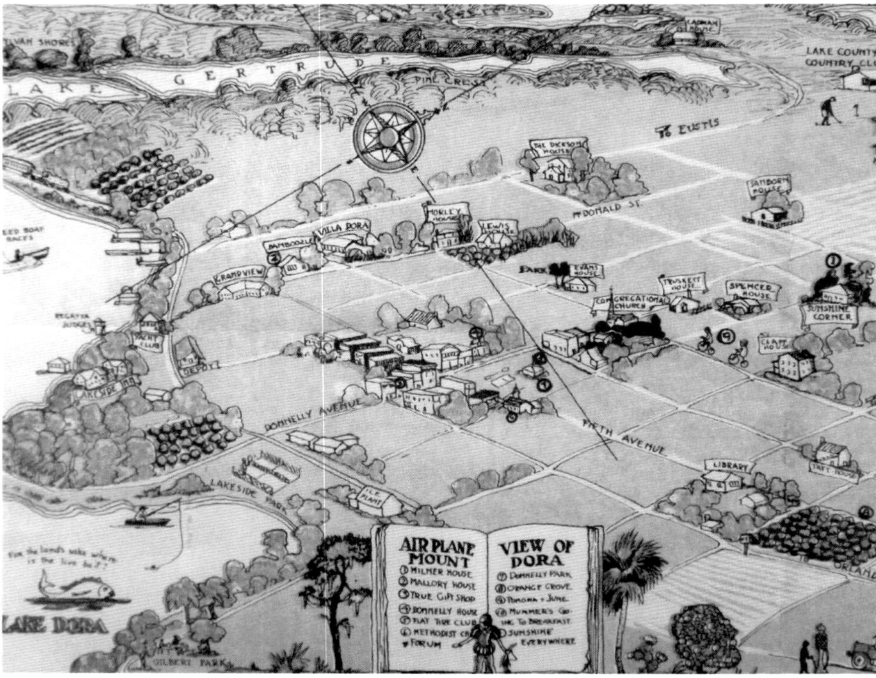

A wonderful (and surprisingly accurate) promotional cartoon map from the 1920s reveals the town's sparse development and a few of its landmark buildings. *Mount Dora Historical Society.*

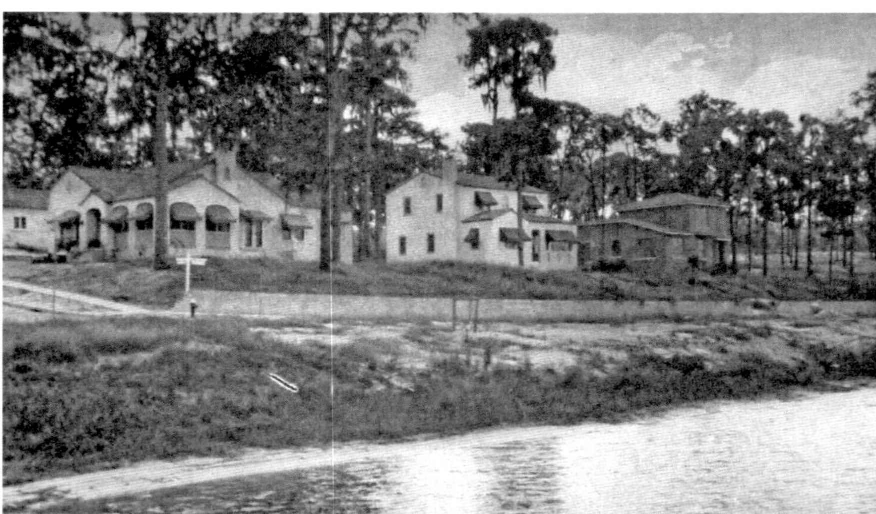

In the 1920s, Lewis R. Heim's dream of creating a community of lovely, lakeside homes came true at Sylvan Shores, at least until the Great Depression hit. *Mount Dora Historical Society.*

"There are no 'ifs' or 'ands' about it," ran one ad. "Mount Dora is to become one of Florida's most important inland cities. This is no dream—those who today mark our words will find we are absolutely right with our judgment." Malone was liberal with his advertising. Any incident could trigger an idea for either a promotion or a reminder to his fellow citizens that Mount Dora's growth depended on everyone and everything. Even the death of an alligator led to a large display ad:

Big Alligator Killed
We are wondering if through the death of this mighty monarch of our local lake
we haven't lost a creature of much interest to our
winter tourists and of no harm to anyone.

A Reward
should be offered to the man who brings about legislation prohibiting the
killing of 'gators. Let's all help to keep Mount Dora and Lake County
as interesting to our Northern friends as possible.

The proliferation of ads and glowing articles promoting Sylvan Shores in the *Mount Dora Topic* were encouraged by the newspaper's owner, who just happened to be none other than Lewis R. Heim. Heim loved to see lead stories under bold headlines such as "20 Homes Soon at Sylvan Shores!" followed a few months later by "Forty-five New Homes at Sylvan Shores." Nearly every issue trumpeted his projects, including the new Sylvan Shores Hotel, which featured a grocery story and barbershop on the ground floor and guest rooms upstairs.

Sales agents were busy, tourists were buying and there was no end in sight.

The Gathering Storm

Heim's success, drive and unbridled enthusiasm soon earned him a position as first vice-president of the Bank of Mount Dora and Trust Company. The bank had been chartered in September 1925 and was about to move into a prime position at the corner of Fifth and Donnelly. Townspeople marveled at the bank's "faultless construction, its elaborate fixtures, and its convenient arrangement" that made it "without question one of the most modern banking rooms in the state."

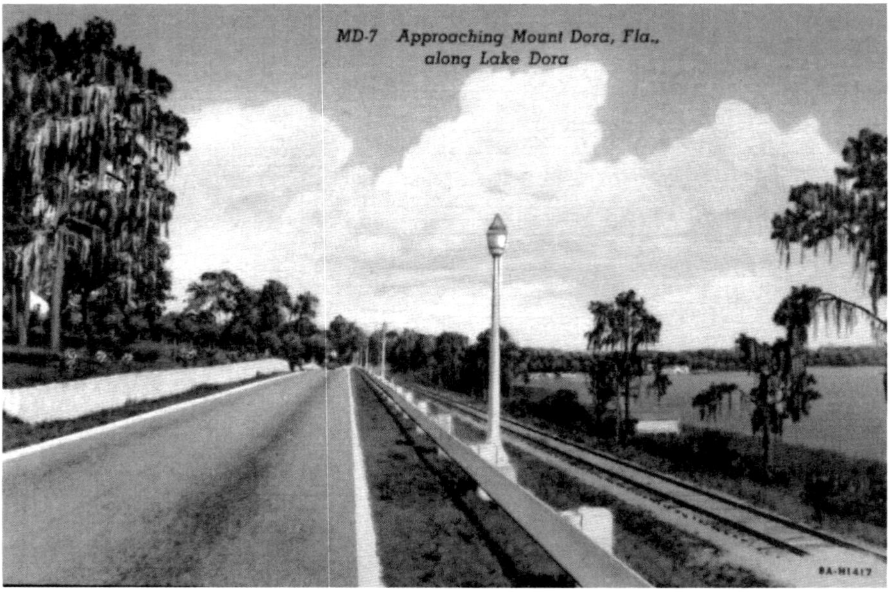

A strand of streetlights contributed by L.R. Heim helped create what was called the "Great White Way" along old Highway 441. *Mount Dora Historical Society.*

Within months of the grand opening of this newest bank, residents were pleased to learn that the collective total of all bank deposits in Mount Dora was $2,350,263.06. Based on Mount Dora's estimated population of two thousand, per capita deposits amounted to $1,175.13 which, according to the local news, "demonstrates that this city is not only one of the most progressive in the state, but also one of the richest according to its population."

Mount Dora was on a roll, but serious storms, both natural and financial, were just around the corner.

In south Florida, the land boom was running at full throttle. The price of lots could rocket from $50 to $10,000 in just months, sometimes changing hands multiple times a day. But that frenzy was drenched on September 17, 1926, when the "No-Name Hurricane" came ashore in Miami. Within hours of making landfall, the storm had taken with it more than five hundred lives and, in today's dollars, left *$165 billion* in property damage. It also halted the unchecked greed of developers and the dreams of get-rich-quick investors. Although some attempted to shore up the land boom, exactly two years later came the one-two punch. On September 16, 1928, an even more devastating hurricane bulldozed its way across south Florida. The winds and rain broke dikes on Lake Okeechobee, and the floodwaters pouring into the lowlands killed an estimated 2,500 people before the storm turned north and rumbled over central Florida and Mount Dora.

As had happened in the wake of the Great Freeze of 1894–95, prospective residents reconsidered investing in a state that was on shaky ground. With the fate of Sylvan Shores on the line, George Malone addressed an ad to Mount Dora's snowbirds:

Homeward Bound!
Homeward Bound Tourists can do a great deal this Spring to dispel the Anti-Florida propaganda which has been infesting the North.

We feel that a thorough inspection of the following properties will give a background for the Truth which Florida deserves.

It concluded with a listing of L.R. Heim's neighborhoods. But these promotions were losing their effectiveness. No amount of advertising could save Mount Dora, the state or the nation from the day of reckoning. Fueled by wealth disparity and the unregulated excess of the 1920s, financial fault lines began to appear in August 1929. But it wasn't until the Wall Street crash on October 24 that the aftershocks of the Great Depression began to ricochet across America.

In Mount Dora, the saga of Sylvan Shores reflected the tenor of the nation. With homebuyers unable to invest, the project fell into disrepair. Vandalized homes, smashed streetlights, overgrown yards and stolen street signs were clear indicators that the Great Depression was hitting home.

Hair-Trigger Tempers in Pistolville

By many accounts, black and white citizens were mutually courteous and respectful in the early years of the town, and Eugene Burley directly credits Mount Dora's white founding families, such as the Donnellys, Simpsons, McDonalds, Tremains, Gilberts and Sadlers, for fostering a sense of trust. Over time, however, two factors would begin to erode the relationships. One was prosperity, and the other was poverty. In the 1920s, when property values began to escalate in the downtown business district, not even the trusted white families could prevent black residents from being removed and relocated—sometimes forcibly—to East Town to make room for new white-owned buildings and businesses.

This was only a sign of things to come as a larger nationwide problem was set to reignite. Although the original Ku Klux Klan had flared up and died out in the 1870s, the organization was reconstituted in the years following World War I. As a rule, Klansmen despised blacks, booze, jazz, sex, immigrants and Catholics and sought to advance and enforce a pure white race, 100 percent Americanism, strict morality, Protestantism and Prohibition. Their message resonated across the country. At its peak in the 1920s, an estimated 5 million Americans had signed up with the Klan, whose members hid beneath white robes and hoods and disguised their hatred with the cross.

In Mount Dora's predominately black East Town, the widespread resurgence of the Klan heightened the already oppressive Jim Crow laws that were specifically designed to keep blacks disenfranchised from society. It also contributed to the social mores working against the residents. Dirt roads, curfews, labor camps for citrus workers and implied boundaries created by untamed vegetation confined residents, who were greatly restricted as to where they lived, socialized and worked. Some were employed at white-owned businesses, many worked for white families as housemaids and yardmen and babysitters and others found physically demanding low-wage employment in orange groves, canneries and sawmills. Some ventured over to a blighted area inhabited by poor whites in the southeast section of town known as "Pistolville." Here, blacks and whites worked side by side at two

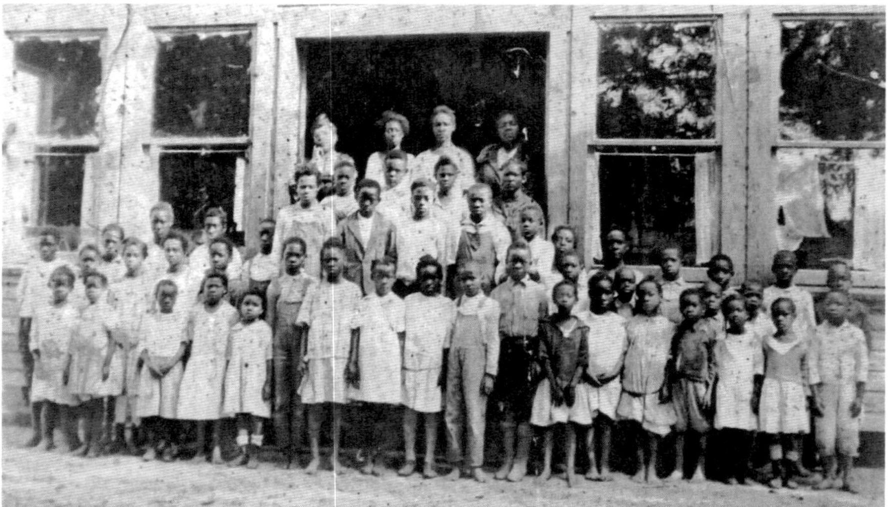

Students gathered at the segregated school held at the Witherspoon Lodge show that Mount Dora's public education was separate but definitely unequal. *Mount Dora Historical Society.*

sawmills during the week, but after dark and on weekends, black workers were quick to return home to avoid Pistolville's favorite pastimes: drinking, brawling and shooting.

It was far safer in East Town, where black entrepreneurs had opened businesses, including food markets, stores, confectioneries, barbershops, civic and fraternal clubs, boardinghouses, churches and dance halls. Yet this sanctuary wasn't always safe. In 1923 at the "salt and pepper" dance club at the Stokely Building, an incident fractured the already fragile alliance between the races. While it was accepted that white men could ask black women to dance, the reverse was taboo. One evening, a white woman stormed out of the club when a black customer invited her to dance. Soon after, Klansmen arrived and killed one of the club's black patrons. The racial conflicts continued the following year when, outside the club, a white man's crude remark toward a black woman proved to be a fatal mistake. He was killed by the woman's brother-in-law, which again led to another visit by members of the KKK.

When the residents of East Town considered the manners of the "good white folks" of downtown, they could only blame "the poor crackers of Pistolville" for the racial divide and misery they were experiencing. Burley described life-and-death games of cat-and-mouse when "night-riding, hood-wearing, lowlife personalities" terrorized East Town. For many black residents, their escape was an undeveloped area called Wolf Branch. "The Wolf Branch area was so vast and quite a jungle," he recalled. "It provided unlimited hiding space. It was a game to hide out, wait for morning and then return home."

Sadly, Mount Dora was beginning to split into two distinct communities. Residents too cautious to leave East Town stayed within neighborhoods where they could live, build, shop and socialize with less fear. In part self-imposed and in part self-preservation, it was a way of life that became natural and, unfortunately, had a tendency to be passed down over generations.

A Gathering Place

In addition to infrastructure, the city in the 1920s also recognized the need to focus on cultural pursuits. With the support of residents, a public auditorium overlooking Donnelly Park was approved. Designed with a Spanish-Mediterranean theme reflective of the times, the Mount Dora Community Building opened in 1929. Even in the depths of the Great Depression, the venue

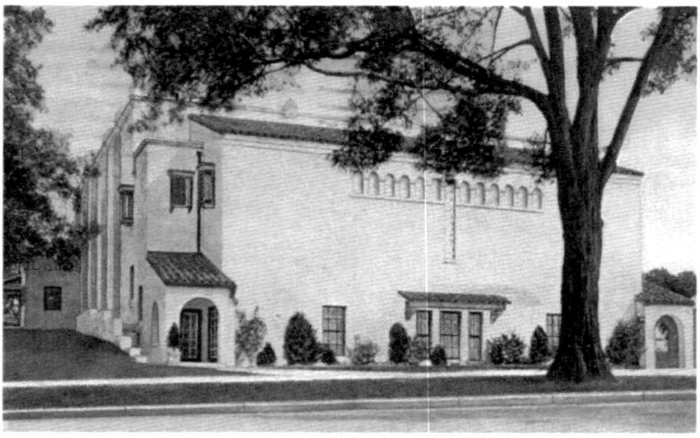

In 1929, the Community Building became the center for Mount Dora's events and activities. *Mount Dora Historical Society.*

remained a point of pride. In a supplement addressed to winter residents, the *Mount Dora Topic* described how the building enhanced the city and the lives of its citizens:

> *Mount Dora Community Building. Erected in 1929 at a cost of more than $40,000, this is situated in the heart of the city overlooking a beautiful park. A large auditorium which will accommodate more than a thousand people and a social room complete with all necessary equipment for having banquets, card parties, and other social gatherings are part of this building. During the tourist season, many delightful entertainments take place in the auditorium. This building is the headquarters for the Mount Dora Tourist Club and other civic organizations.*

A Mind Is a Wonderful Thing: Milner, Rosenwald and Cauley Lott

Mount Dora's first school opened in 1881 and was available to the town's black children only when white students were not using it. A separate one-room schoolhouse for black students opened in 1886, but after it was destroyed by fire in 1922, the historic Witherspoon Masonic Lodge served as a temporary school, with classes held on the ground floor.

Over the next three years, parents and community leaders raised money to build a new school before receiving a helping hand from two distinct but like-minded benefactors. In 1926, Jewish philanthropist Julius Rosenwald—then president of Sears & Roebuck—and Civil War veteran/Presbyterian minister Duncan Milner provided $13,000 each to build a permanent four-room school: the Milner-Rosenwald Academy.

Closely associated with the school was Cauley O. Lott, the son of a Georgia sharecropper who held a bachelor's degree from Florida A&M University and a master's degree from the University of Pittsburgh. He served as the school's principal from 1938 until integrated schools went into effect in 1970. He later became the first African American elected to the city council. Cauley Lott Memorial Park, located at Highland Street and Pine Avenue, was named in his honor.

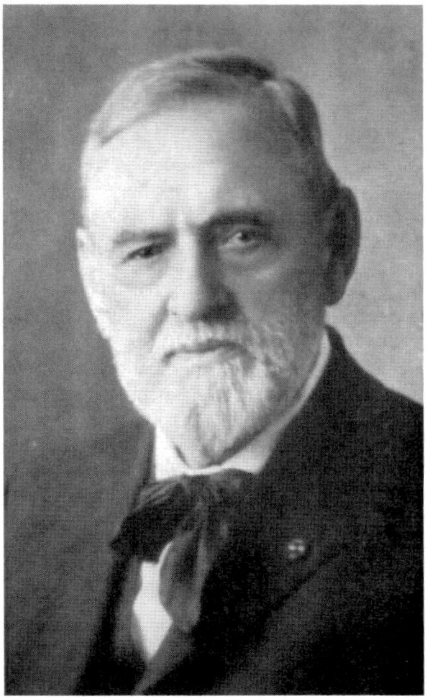

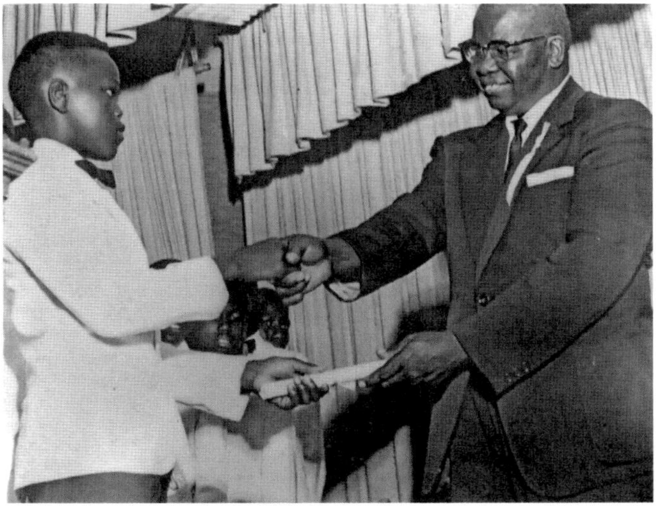

Top: Reverend Duncan Milner (shown) and Sears & Roebuck president Julius Rosenwald contributed $13,000 each to launch the Milner-Rosenwald Academy in 1926. It would remain the primary school for the black community until integration went into effect in 1970. *Mount Dora Historical Society.*

Bottom: Cauley O. Lott was considered one of the most respected educators and active citizens in the history of Mount Dora. *Mount Dora Historical Society.*

Chapter 10
NEVER GIVE UP

We must take time to pay honorable loyalty to society, and be a real community.
—Peter Tomasello

When Calvin Came Calling

Just a few weeks into the 1930s, the town kicked off the decade with an event that was one of the high-water marks in its history.

In his book *Presidents in Florida*, historian Jim Clark explained that after leaving office, Calvin Coolidge decided to enjoy an extended stay in central Florida for several reasons—first to enjoy the weather, then to dedicate Bok Tower in Lake Wales and then to spend a month at the Lakeside Inn before traveling to Orlando to spend time with a cousin.

Aside from dedicating new additions to the Lakeside Inn and attending services at the Congregational Church, the former president was reticent to accept invitations to anything. In fact, he reportedly threatened to leave town if people didn't stop asking him to participate in civic activities. Former first lady Grace Coolidge was more sporting. Accepting an invitation by the Garden Club to plant a Portuguese silver cypress chosen for its potential height (one hundred feet) and lifespan (one hundred years), she joined a procession of club members carrying baskets of flowers and flame vines to the newly opened Mount Dora Community Building. It was a momentous occasion. On hand to greet

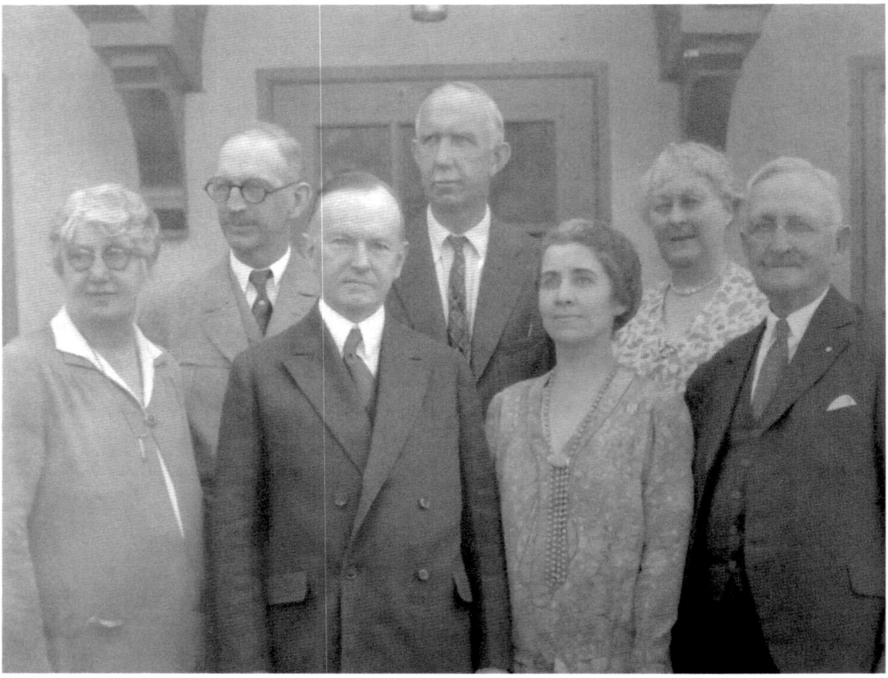

Former president Calvin Coolidge was the special guest at the dedication of new wings at the Lakeside Inn in January 1930. Apparently, the former president was the only one aware someone had a camera. *Mount Dora Historical Society.*

Mrs. Coolidge were town officials, a troop of Girl Scouts and schoolchildren singing "America the Beautiful," and also Boy Scout troops, including Ben Heath, who opened the ceremony with a fanfare on his bugle.

As the last notes floated across neighboring Donnelly Park, Mrs. Coolidge was handed the ceremonial shovel that triggered the first of many ovations. As reported in the *Mount Dora Topic*, "Mrs. Coolidge's acceptance of the shovel and her energetic use of it was enthusiastically applauded, and was accompanied by the clicking of many cameras. [She] cast the first shovelful of dirt around the roots, and followed it by a vigorous wielding of the implement until all of the roots were well covered."

With the roots well covered, Garden Club president Mrs. R.C. Conklin stepped forward to offer a few appropriate and clearly well-rehearsed remarks. With a commanding voice, Mrs. Conklin addressed the crowd, commenting that she "felt sure the tree would grow as Mrs. Coolidge had proven herself a good planter, for she had already planted herself deeply in the hearts of the people."

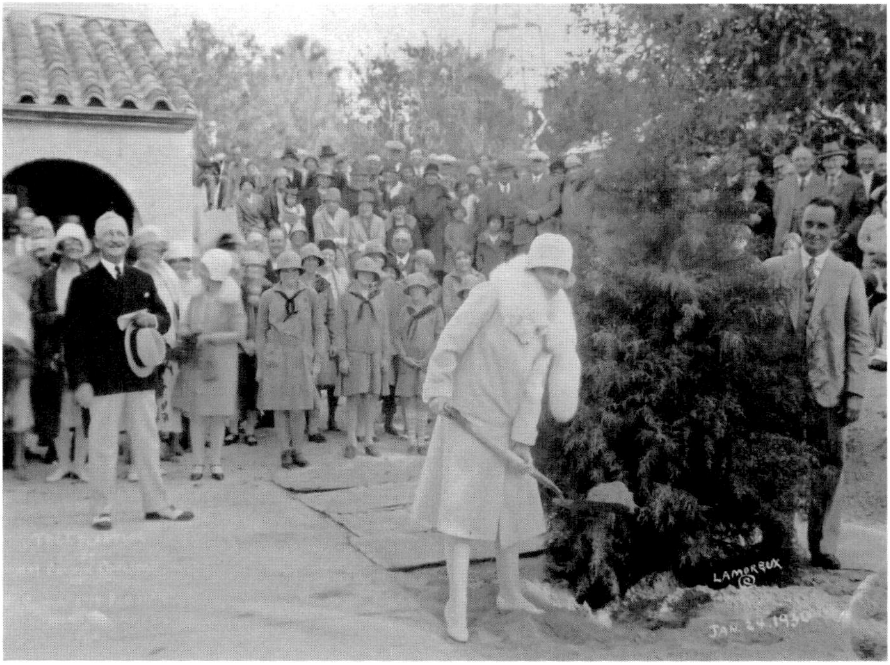

A highlight in Mount Dora history came in January 1930, when former first lady Grace Coolidge planted a Portuguese silver cypress tree beside the Community Building. *Mount Dora Historical Society.*

When the ceremony ended, the shovel was affixed with a plaque to note its importance. Today, the remains of the Portuguese silver cypress lay beneath the city hall parking lot.

BUY HERE, PAY HERE

Even as the Coolidges were planting trees and dedicating buildings in Mount Dora, the nation was dealing with a hangover triggered by the excesses of the 1920s. The Great Depression had arrived. In 1932, President Hoover's halting reactions to the economic collapse stood in contrast with that of his challenger, Franklin Delano Roosevelt. While campaigning for the presidency in May 1932, FDR told students and faculty at Atlanta's Oglethorpe University, "It is common sense to take a method and try it. If it fails, admit it frankly and try another. But above all, try *something*."

Elected in November 1932 and sworn in the following March, FDR's first one hundred days set the stage for the New Deal. There were programs to provide government jobs for the unemployed; tougher regulations applied to Wall Street, banks and transportation; and assistance was offered to farmers and small businesses to boost economic growth. In October 1933, Roosevelt introduced a plan giving small municipalities financial assistance to build generating plants. Mount Dora jumped on the offer and applied for a loan with the government. Although the idea was generally supported at first, delays in the process gave some residents time to question the city's wisdom of building its own light and power plant. Opposing views formed, leading to one of the rare moments when a contentious issue was fought in public. George Malone, highly regarded as one of the town's leading salesmen, applied his skills of gentle persuasion to oppose the project. Focused on the city's finances, he wrote an open letter to his fellow citizens. "True enough it would be very nice to own our own light plant," he offered. "But, my friends, this is no time to burden ourselves with additional obligations. Now is the time to pay our debt if humanly possible."

Pushing hard for the plant and using capitals for emphasis, the opposition took out a full-page ad: "You don't want your water and light rates increased, do you?" it asked. "Why don't You vote for Your benefit by casting a vote in favor of a municipal plant in Mount Dora? Without it the future action will be an almost certain increase in Your bills!"

Ultimately, the city was wary of taking on the financial burden. Instead of investing in a new power plant, the city negotiated lower rates from its current provider. While the issue had placed residents on opposing sides, it demonstrated that the town's 1,600 residents were able to disagree and then move forward with a shared sense of purpose.

This attitude didn't go unnoticed by Florida's Speaker of the House, Peter Tomasello, who was invited to address the annual meeting of the Mount Dora Chamber of Commerce. "If we are part of a community, we cannot live entirely to ourselves," he declared to the rapt audience. "We must take time to pay honorable loyalty to society, and be a real community. A group has a common purpose through coherence of effort and the living up to an ideal of fraternity and friendship."

Tomasello's motivational address resonated with the residents, and the ideal of fraternity was strengthened. Although the national unemployment rate had fallen from a brutal 24.75 percent to a still shocking 21.4 percent, civic leaders realized that for recovery to really take hold it was critical

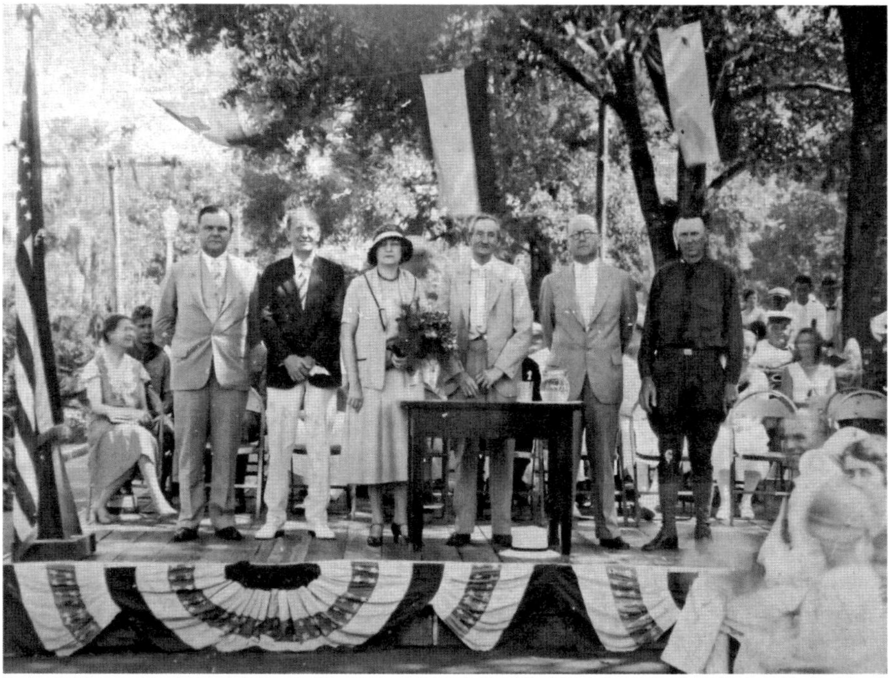

Mount Dora has been a popular stop for visiting politicians. In 1931, former governor John W. Martin (1925–29), *at left*, joined the mayor and town dignitaries at the Fourth of July celebration in Annie Donnelly Park. *Mount Dora Historical Society.*

to support local businesses. Foreshadowing the "Shop Local" movement that would gain strength during the Great Recession of 2008, the month after Tomasello's visit merchants coordinated a twelve-week "Trade at Home Campaign" promoted by the chamber of commerce. The *Mount Dora Topic* added to the drive with a none-too-subtle hint to boost local sales:

Whose Rent Do You Pay?

Are you helping pay the rent
of the big city stores?

Are you contributing to the taxes, insurance, interest, employees' wages,
and the hundreds of other big expenses of the out of town
stores or mail order houses?

Most surely you are if you are
buying anything from them.

Isn't it better to buy from the
merchants of your town?

You pay no more, and your money stays
where it will be invested for your own good.

Buy It in Our Town

In addition to patronizing local businesses, Mount Dora was investing in itself through new buildings, businesses and civic projects. At the junction of the "Golden Triangle"—where connecting roads led to Mount Dora, Tavares and Eustis—developers of the Riley Tourist Camp invested $25,000 to create a neighborhood of stone cottages and recreational facilities that, at the time, were considered the "most modern and up-to-date tourist facility in the state of Florida." In town, FDR's Works Progress Administration put $30,000 toward the construction of a public school auditorium and added

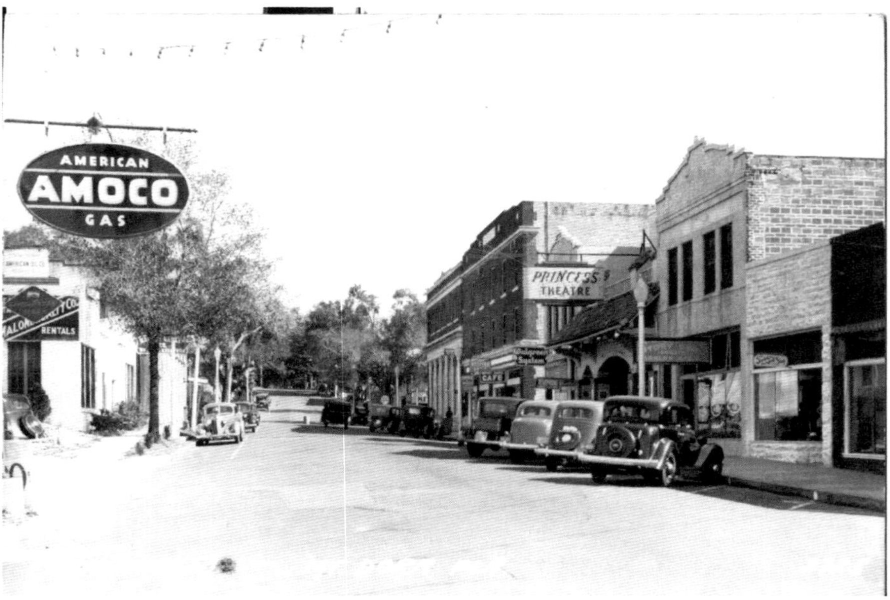

Looking east from the intersection of Alexander Street and Fifth Avenue, a gas station, a theater, a market and a café are the hallmarks of a small town. *Mount Dora Historical Society.*

another $5,000 toward improvements to the Lawn Bowling Club and Evans Park. Even Donnelly Park's popular shuffleboard courts received a $600 makeover. But most residents agreed that the best investment arrived via the Florida Telephone Corporation. Following $20,000 in improvements and upgrades, residents no longer had to crank a phone and wait for an operator. The town's antiquated telephone exchange was converted into the "modern dial type telephone system," and Mount Dora was now just one call away from the world.

Those Were the Days

During the 1930s, writers and photographers combed the nation to chronicle people and places as part of a Works Progress Administration project. Mostly accurate, this 1935 description of Mount Dora has stood the test of time:

> *Mount Dora (107 alt., 1,613 pop.), founded in 1882, rises in successive terraces from the shores of the lake. The broad streets overlooking the water are shaded by oaks, magnolia, and a variety of palms. The neat white frame houses, set back in ample lawns, give the town the appearance of a quiet New England village. Mount Dora has long been a rendezvous for yachting and outboard motor enthusiasts. Lake Dora and other lakes are connected by canals, and it is possible to reach the Atlantic Ocean by inland waterways via the Ocklawaha and St. Johns Rivers. The yacht club, one of the oldest in Florida, holds annual regattas here during February.*
>
> *The South Florida Chautauqua at Mount Dora, established in the 1880s, was one of the first in the South. The assembly grounds and auditorium were in a tract of virgin forest between Lakes Dora and Gertrude, a site now known as Sylvan Shores, a residential development. The Chautauqua was abandoned shortly after 1905 when the auditorium was destroyed by fire.*
>
> *In Donnelly Park, adjoining the business district, are a large municipal auditorium and recreational grounds.*

The Winds of War

In June 1939, Mount Dora resident Major Thomas H. Cooley returned home from a visit to Washington, D.C., and told his fellow citizens that there were no immediate plans for a general mobilization of the organized reserves but rather "improvement of the national defense, so far as law permits, is going ahead. The reserves won't be called unless there is a change in the situation in Europe." That change would come within months.

On September 1, 1939, Germany invaded Poland, and World War II was on. Suddenly, small-town Mount Dora had a larger worldview. Residents could handicap the war by reviewing charts that listed the air strength, troop strength, naval power and resources of Britain, France, Germany, Poland, Russia and Italy. With an eye on Europe, locals were aware that the war could, and likely would, reach America. World affairs were clearly on the mind of the community when, on May 29, 1941, the *Mount Dora Topic* reprinted a copy of President Roosevelt's National Emergency Declaration

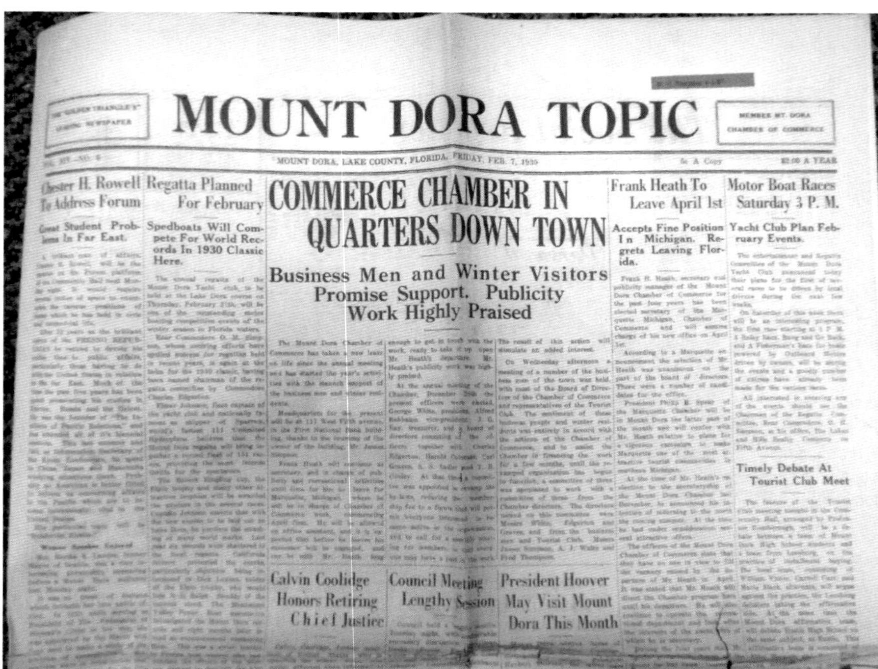

MOUNT DORA TOPIC

Chester H. Rowell To Address Forum

Regatta Planned For February

Speedboats Will Compete For World Records In 1930 Classic Here.

COMMERCE CHAMBER IN QUARTERS DOWN TOWN

Business Men and Winter Visitors Promise Support. Publicity Work Highly Praised

Frank Heath To Leave April 1st

Accepts Fine Position In Michigan. Regrets Leaving Florida.

Motor Boat Races Saturday 3 P. M.

Yacht Club Plan February Events.

Timely Debate At Tourist Club Meet

Calvin Coolidge Honors Retiring Chief Justice

Council Meeting Lengthy Session

President Hoover May Visit Mount Dora This Month

This 1936 edition of the *Mount Dora Topic* shows its wide range of coverage. For decades, it was the main source of news for the community, covering notable people, winter visitors, civic groups, social events, East Town, schools and even national and international news. *Nancy Howell.*

and alerted every man, woman and child over fifteen years old to attend a "National Defense Mass Meeting" that evening.

"The defense problem is not a local one," read the article. "The leaders of other nations have forced upon us a situation not of our own making which we must meet now and overcome…It is not whether you are war-minded or a pacifist; you cannot evade the crisis which faces this great nation of ours…It is your duty as an American to be in hand…You have a part in the defense set up of the Nation and you must assume your individual responsibility."

Not yet at war but not truly at peace, it was an unusual time in America and Mount Dora. In an effort to maintain an air of normalcy, Mount Dora continued to pitch itself to outsiders as a natural, healthy destination. By the fall of 1941, the chamber of commerce was comfortable casting a line for winter travelers. But it wasn't just visitors it was seeking—it was also looking for permanent residents. The pride of owning a home in Mount Dora was promoted through alliterative advertorials: "How would you like to live in an orange grove? To enjoy a June day in January, under a cloudless, blue-vaulted sky; to encounter a balmy breeze fragrantly freighted with a bouquet breath of a million orange blossoms?"

As it turned out, this idyllic vision would have to wait, as more important matters demanded attention. Just weeks later, an attack on Pearl Harbor found America joining the Allies and Mount Dora joining the fight. Local newspapers replaced pictures of gardens and shuffleboard courts with graphics that showed the size of the American naval fleet and distances between war zones in the South Pacific. Local businesses, including the First National Bank, pledged their support:

For the National Defense

Never has the United States failed in an emergency.
We are young enough, tough enough,
smart enough to meet any crisis.

As industry joins Government in preparing armaments
to give power-mad dictators pause—banks will be called up
to finance raw materials, machinery, plants, and payrolls.

Banking is ready. And we're eager to do our part.

During World War II, thousands of young men from across Lake County ended up overseas; many would never return. On the homefront, some residents volunteered for the Red Cross, while others learned to identify enemy aircraft and serve as "airplane spotters" in the event a Japanese Zero reached Lake Dora. They supported the war effort through scrap drives and by planting Victory Gardens. They invested in bonds at drives like the one in 1944 that drew large crowds to Donnelly Park with the display of a German 88mm howitzer and a Messerschmitt fighter plane captured from the enemy.

Meanwhile, up in Connecticut, former resident L.R. Heim, whose dream of completing Sylvan Shores was interrupted by the Great Depression, was making news and aiding the war effort by inventing innovative products to improve the performance of America's airplanes, as well as rebuilding his fortune by producing much-needed ball bearings with the "Heim Centerless Cylindrical Roll Grinder."

The combined effort of America and its Allies led to victory in Europe. On May 8, 1945, Boy Scouts fanned out across the city to distribute copies of Mayor Simpson's proclamation declaring a town holiday. With businesses shuttered, crowds gathered at Donnelly Park for the V-E Day celebration, which began with five blasts of the fire siren and included President Truman's live radio broadcast played over loudspeakers. Three months

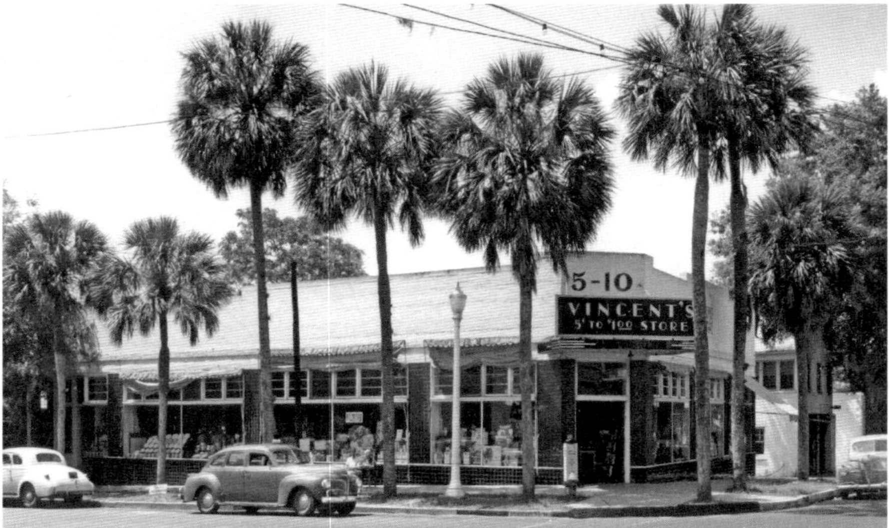

In the 1940s, as in many towns across the nation, a five and dime was the cornerstone among Mount Dora's downtown shops. *Mount Dora Historical Society.*

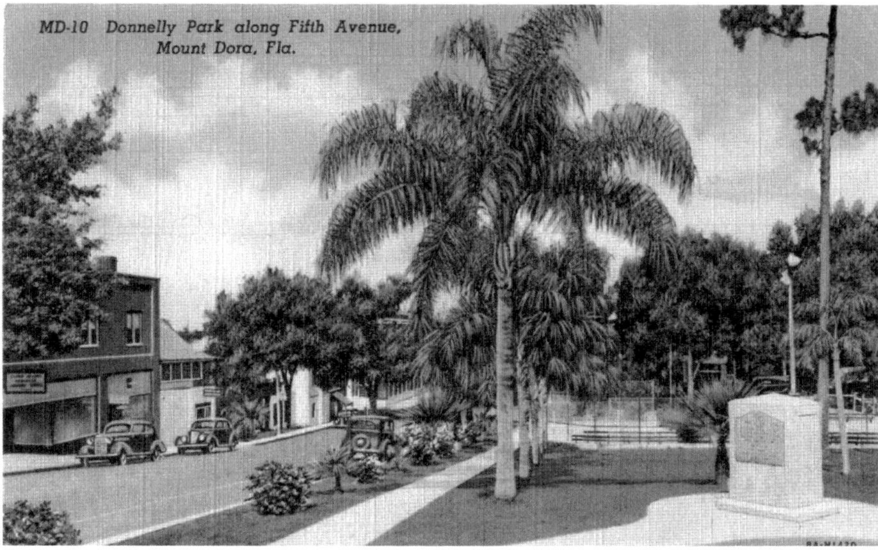

This idyllic image from the past is, incredibly, reflective of the present. Note the war memorial in the foreground. *Mount Dora Historical Society.*

later, townspeople returned to Donnelly Park to mark V-J Day in a more somber tone. The mayor invited his fellow citizens to "show our humble appreciation for victory by joining in this simple ceremony," which included a prayer of thanksgiving followed by a brief parade and a touching service.

"Now Mount Dora mothers and fathers, wives and sweethearts, await the arrival of their loved ones, thank God!" wrote the *Topic*. "All is very quiet on the homefront."

FACING FORWARD

The 1940s ended with Mount Dora enjoying the peace that victory had promised. A real estate boom that began during the last months of the war reminded longtime residents of a similar surge in the 1920s. This time, however, it was prompted not by speculators but rather by actual buyers, who purchased homes to live in, and confident retailers, who opened new businesses.

To demonstrate how far the city had traveled in its first four decades, the Mount Dora Chamber of Commerce joined the Florida Advertising Commission in a study to inventory the town's assets. The report concluded that Mount Dora's main industry was tourism, although a sawmill, a cement plant and a fertilizer factory also contributed to the local economy. The police force consisted of one car and three officers, and a fire department employed one full-time firefighter supported by a dozen volunteers.

There were three schools for white children (elementary, junior high and high school) and one school for black children. In the groves and fields, growers were raising citrus, watermelons, celery, lettuce, cabbage and beans. Unskilled workers received $0.65 per hour, while skilled black and white males received $1.00 per hour. In comparison, skilled white females earned $0.75, while skilled black females took home $0.65 for each hour of labor.

The First National Bank had recovered from the Great Depression, and deposits had reached $3.6 million. Retail was prospering as well. There were six hotels (four year-round and two seasonal) and four restaurants, and downtown had nearly two dozen stores—not a single vacancy. Citizens were active in ten civic clubs and had their choice of five churches to attend every Sunday.

Having outlasted a Great Depression and a world war, Mount Dora was on the rebound and looking forward to the 1950s.

Chapter 11

ON ROADS, RACE AND RADIATION

The only thing wrong with your neighborhood is the Reeses.
–Sheriff Willis McCall

ONE FOR THE ROAD

Thanks to its sunny beaches and balmy winters, Florida in the 1950s was well on its way to becoming one of the country's favorite vacation destinations. But some of the roads in the pre-interstate era were scarcely capable of supporting the many tourists who migrated south each year. In central Florida, a portion of the original Dixie Highway (aka Highway 441) between Ocala and Orlando was being stretched to its limits. Where the road rolled through Mount Dora's business district, traffic got tricky—especially when commercial vehicles tried to navigate the narrow lanes or accidents blocked the roadway. It was just as bad outside of town, where drivers traveled a single-lane brick road before joining up with Orlando's Orange Blossom Trail.

The decision to construct what locals would call the "new" Highway 441 led to one of the biggest disagreements in Mount Dora history. But it was a showdown that ended with a decision that literally saved the heart of the city. Although residents agreed that a new road was necessary, determining exactly where it would go was elusive. Only a handful of realistic alternatives were possible. During the planning stages, one early concept plowed a highway through the center of town along Fifth Avenue, another would run parallel to the railroad tracks and then the leading contender was an eighty-foot-wide, four-lane road several blocks north and east of the commercial district. Projected to accommodate an estimated fifteen thousand cars daily, proponents of this route offered that the increased traffic would bring potential customers to their shops and restaurants. Opponents countered that building a highway of this magnitude would mean razing fourteen feet of abutting property as well as 153 mature trees along Fifth Avenue and Highland Street.

In a 1993 interview, downtown hardware store owner Sonny Rehbaum explained the predicament. "Businessmen and bankers thought the community would collapse if the highway was put outside the city. Others thought it would destroy the city if it came through. But no one had anything to compare it to. They were all trying to decide what was right."

During planning sessions to discuss alternatives, supporters of the "highway through the heart of town" had the advantage, but it didn't last long. Not only was George White, who served as president of both the First

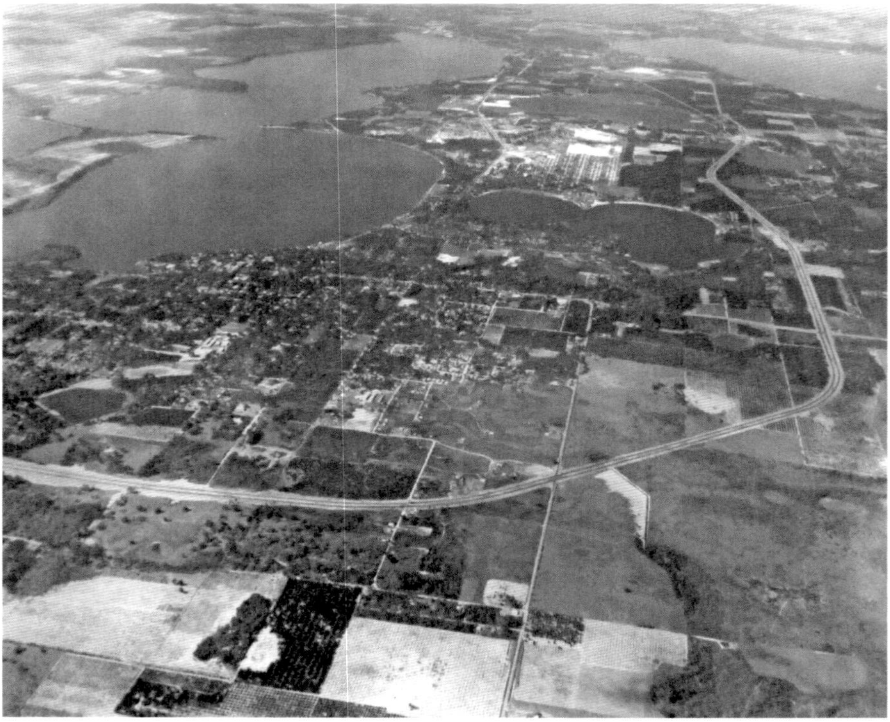

An aerial view shows how the wide arc of the redirected Highway 441 preserved the heart of town, seen below the lake on the left. *Lake County Historical Society.*

National Bank and the chamber of commerce, against the intrusion of the road, but the opposition didn't realize that they were also facing an opponent with an ace up his sleeve. At several meetings with transportation officials, Richard Edgerton spoke for like-minded citizens when he told them that the road through the business district would destroy not just city hall and Donnelly Park but, far more importantly, the character of Mount Dora. To some, Edgerton's stand seemed at odds with his self-interests. At the time, he was the owner of the Lakeside Inn and stood to benefit from a stream of traffic bringing thousands of guests within blocks of his hotel. But Edgerton looked beyond the short-term easy fix with an eye on the future.

Not only was he holding the high ground, he was also holding the position as the State of Florida's hotel and restaurant commissioner. And there was another very important factor that gave his words extra weight: Edgerton and his wife, Marie, just happened to be close friends with Governor LeRoy Collins and his wife, Mary. After making little headway with Department of Transportation officials at public meetings, Edgerton picked up the phone and placed a call to the governor. The rest, as they say, is history.

Not long after he hung up with the governor, transportation officials returned to Mount Dora with plans for a new road that would bypass the village. The proposed road would follow an easement through orange groves on the town's northern perimeter. More importantly, with the highway and the lake creating buffer zones, it would keep urban sprawl well outside the town center.

Even though the new plan was approved, it didn't seem like a victory for Edgerton or the downtown merchants at first. As opponents had claimed, the road routed travelers (and their money) away from the downtown shops and restaurants, as well as the Lakeside Inn. It would take nearly three decades before Edgerton and his colleagues could fully realize the good they had accomplished.

Living in a Black-and-White World

As some residents were preoccupied with the routing of a new highway, others were more concerned with entering a new era of equality. In Mount Dora, as throughout the South, segregation was present everywhere: schools, restaurants, stores, churches, swimming pools, neighborhoods, movie theaters and water fountains. Downtown's Princess Theatre had two entrances: one that led to a whites-only main floor and a second that led black citizens to the balcony via a side stairway.

Yet even in the wake of *Brown v. Board of Education*, when the concept of "separate but equal" was ruled unconstitutional, some residents wanted to maintain the status quo of inequality. The *Mount Dora Herald*, a pro-segregation newspaper, was launched in reaction to the *Mount Dora Topic*'s more racially tolerant perspective. It enlisted Cauley Lott, principal of the black-only Milner-Rosenwald Academy, to pen an op-ed feature titled, "How the Educated Negro Feels Toward Integration." He noted, "95% of the negroes are satisfied with the efforts to give the negro equal facilities. As long as the state gives us separate but equal facilities we are content to let the situation remain as is…Since the white man owns most of the things the colored man depends on, we feel that we must respect each other."

While his words served the *Herald*'s motives and were clearly rooted in the mindset of the times, they were spoken at a time when the case of the Groveland Four was still fresh in the memory of Lake County residents. The tragedy that would engage future Supreme Court justice Thurgood Marshall began in the summer of 1949 when a white teenage girl accused four local black men of rape. As a result, one of the four, Ernest Thomas, was quickly hunted down and killed by a one-thousand-man posse led by Lake County's Sheriff Willis McCall. To coerce confessions from the three remaining suspects, McCall and his deputies took them to a makeshift torture chamber hidden in the basement of the Lake County Courthouse in neighboring Tavares. After the men recovered from beatings that fractured bones and dislodged teeth, their trial ended with Walter Irvin and Samuel Shepherd being sent to Death Row, while sixteen-year-old Charles Greenlee was sentenced to life.

After the United States Supreme Court ordered a retrial for Irvin and Shepherd, on November 6, 1951, McCall volunteered to transfer the two from the state prison in Raiford back to the jail in Tavares. En route, McCall pulled over on a dark country road near Umatilla, ordered his handcuffed passengers out of the car and, without warning, shot the two men, killing Shepherd and critically wounding Irvin with two shots in the chest and one through his neck. The transparency of the slaughter made news around the world. Even worse for McCall, it turned the owner and editor of the *Mount Dora Topic* against him. Mabel Norris Reese had once been a champion of McCall's, but now her articles and editorials called

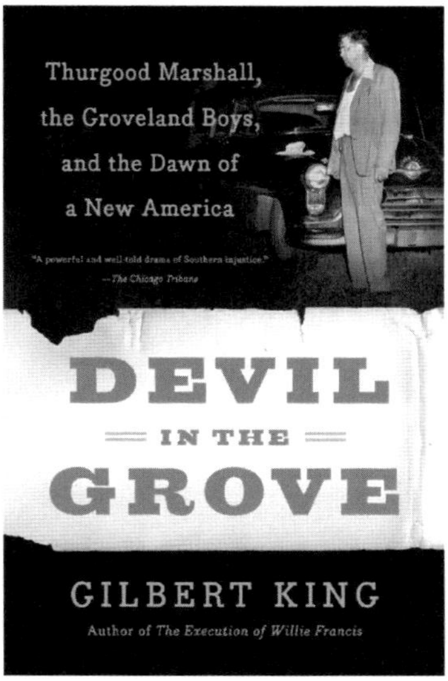

Gilbert King's Pulitzer Prize–winning book details the case of the Groveland Four, as well as its impact on Mount Dora. *Author's collection.*

To learn more about this case and a sorrowful period in Mount Dora (and Florida) history, read Gilbert King's *Devil in the Grove: Thurgood Marshall, the Groveland Boys, and the Dawn of a New America*, which received multiple literary awards including the 2013 Pulitzer Prize for general nonfiction. In an interview with the authors, King described how the case had been wrapped in silence for more than half a century.

"Many people now in their 60s and 70s who were young then tell me almost unanimously they didn't know this was going on and their parents never told them about it. But this became a huge civil rights case. Thurgood Marshall came down here and the case was on the front page of countless newspapers across the country and overseas. Yet even in this county where something big like this happened, people didn't want to talk about it.

"It's been an awakening for people who've read this book. They feel inspired to write me and tell me it opened up dialogues within their household. Sometimes feelings are still raw, but some people are coming to terms with their parents and grandparents about what it was like in Lake County and really, what it was like in a great part of the South."—Gilbert King

www.gilbertking.com

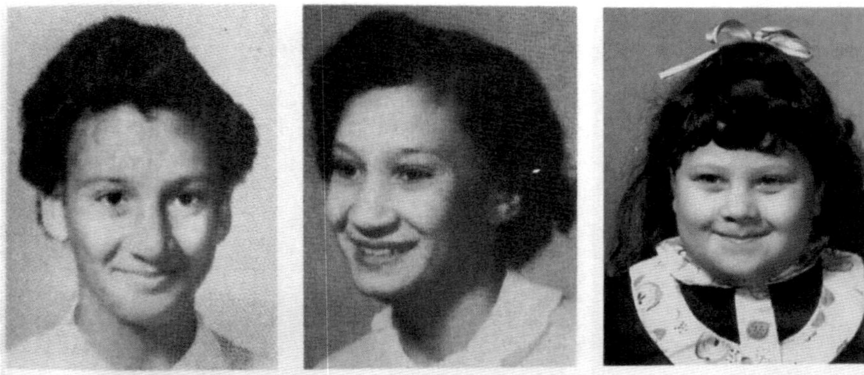

Ester Platt Laura Platt Violet Platt

Shown are three of the five Platt children. Suspected of being "negroes," the five students gained international attention when they were kicked out of Mount Dora's white public schools. *Mount Dora Historical Society.*

him out for his unrepentant violence. Her opposition didn't sit well with the sheriff or his supporters. McCall put pressure on the *Topic*'s clients to cancel their ads.

The sheriff's vendetta against Reese and the *Mount Dora Topic* was followed by another racial incident. On the heels of the tragic case of the Groveland Four came the saga of Mount Dora's Platt family.

Allan and Laura Platt along with their children relocated from South Carolina in the fall of 1954. Several of the Platt children were enrolled in Mount Dora public schools until classmates, teachers and parents looked at their skin and facial features and began to suspect that they were not actually of Croatan Indian and Irish descent, as they claimed, but were actually "negroes" and therefore ineligible to attend whites-only schools.

Working on a hunch, McCall arrived at the Platt home one evening, lined up the frightened children and, in a rudimentary examination, had their skin photographed and the shape of their noses checked before declaring them to be black. He advised their parents to enroll the children at the blacks-only Milner-Rosenwald Academy, a decision supported by the principal, superintendent and school board. But Allan Platt, who also believed that "blacks had their place," refused. Once again, a Mount Dora story made news around the world.

On December 13, 1954, the Platts were featured in a two-page spread in *Time* magazine. Mr. Platt wrote to Governor Collins, requesting that he intercede on his family's behalf. Collins declined, saying that it was a local matter. As the situation dragged on, tempers rose and the Platts were forced to leave their rented home after vigilantes threatened to torch it.

Then the family found a champion: Mabel Norris Reese.

Continuing to confront McCall in print, Reese again angered the sheriff by siding with the Platts. Sympathetic attorneys shared her position and offered the family pro bono services, while others contributed to a legal defense fund. Mount Dora's Christian Home and Bible School came forward and invited the children to receive a free education on its campus—a gesture of kindness that led McCall to threaten the school with a lawsuit.

Across town, a collective example of moral support was demonstrated when more than sixty students at the whites-only Mount Dora High School signed a petition in support of the Platts that was then mailed to the editors of *Time* magazine. The backlash of the petition, some from parents but more so from other students, came quickly. One student who signed the petition recalls arriving at school the following morning to see a chalk line dividing the sidewalk into separate lanes—one for "Whites Only" and the other for "N----- Lovers." He bravely chose to back up his signature by walking the "black" lane.

Eventually, the Platt case would go to trial. On October 18, 1955, the circuit court decided that the Platt children were white and, therefore, entitled to attend Mount Dora's white schools. Weeks later, the *Topic* quoted the unrepentant sheriff, who implied that his background had blessed him with unique insights in analyzing racial composition: "I was raised on a farm," he boasted. "I can tell a stalk of yellow corn from white corn; rutabagas from turnips; sweet potatoes from Irish potatoes; a Hereford bull from a Black Angus bull."

Reese, on the other hand, had been raised with values and courage. Whether it was the case of the Groveland Four or the Platt family, she continued to confront McCall and press for truth and justice. Her efforts came with repercussions. Red crosses and "KKK" were painted on the windows of her business, dead fish were dumped on the lawn of her Sylvan Shores home, crosses were burned in her yard, her dog was poisoned and, in March 1956, two bombs were detonated at her house.

Disgusted at the lawlessness that had reached Sylvan Shores, one of Reese's neighbors met with the sheriff to tell him it was wrong not to provide their neighborhood with more protection in the wake of residential terrorism. "The only thing wrong with your neighborhood is the Reeses," McCall replied.

Mabel Norris Reese would eventually leave Mount Dora, but not before receiving honors and awards—including a Pulitzer Prize nomination—for her articles and editorials on the Platt family. Mount Dora's schools would not be integrated until 1970, although McCall's reign would continue uninterrupted until April 1972. The final straw came when he was indicted for second-degree murder in the death of Tommy Vickers, a mentally disabled African American prisoner who had been kicked and beaten to death in his jail cell. Suspended from office by Governor Reuben Askew during his trial, McCall was acquitted by an all-white jury and returned to office. Months later, he was defeated for reelection; his twenty-eight-year reign had ended. He died at his Umatilla home in 1994.

Burning Issue

In August 1954, the Ku Klux Klan paid yet another visit to East Town. As Mabel Norris Reese noted in an editorial, the reaction of its black residents to the domestic terrorists was in contrast with a similar event that had occurred several years earlier: "Mount Dora's colored community was not cowed by the demonstration this time. Residents there did not retreat behind closed doors or take off to the scrub lands as they did when the Klan paraded through in 1948. Instead, they took another attitude. They were unafraid, and they were resentful."

Alas, Mount Dora

It was clearly a curious time to be a child in Mount Dora. In addition to learning that the Constitution provided blacks and whites with equal privileges, students were also being taught they could survive a nuclear attack by learning how to "duck and cover" beneath their desks.

Part of the threat of an atomic war affecting Mount Dora could be traced to its location. Fifty miles east at Cape Canaveral, a new space center was being constructed, and thirty miles away in Orlando a front-line Strategic Air Command center was operating at the McCoy Air Force Base. Just a missile's flight away in Havana, Fidel Castro was establishing a friendly relationship with the Soviet Union.

Bringing the threat of nuclear attack even closer to home was writer and novelist Pat Frank. The author of the apocalyptic 1959 novel *Alas, Babylon** lived in neighboring Tangerine on the shores of Lake Ola, just a few miles from Mount Dora. Frank had put fictional Fort Repose (inspired by Mount Dora) center stage in a doomsday scenario. When America's government and most of Florida's major cities are destroyed in a nuclear battle between the United States and the USSR, Fort Repose/Mount Dora was one of the few surviving towns in a state considered a "contaminated zone."

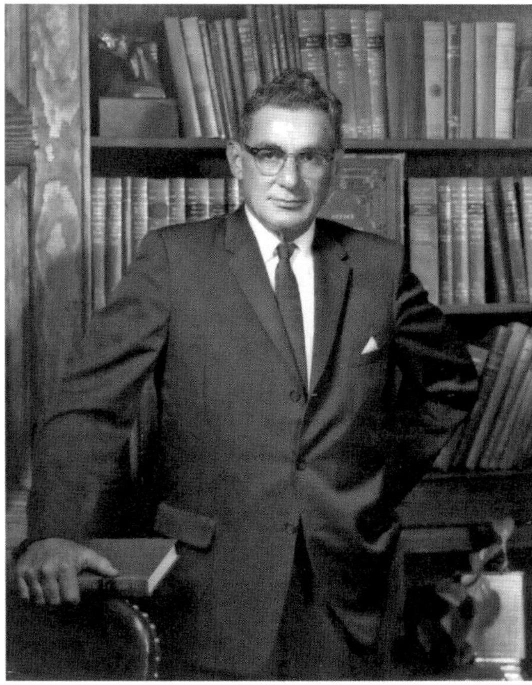

In 1959, local author Pat Frank put Mount Dora (aka Fort Repose) in the center of a nuclear Armageddon in his classic *Alas, Babylon*.

Within a year of its publication, *Alas, Babylon* would cause a headache for CBS. The network had planned to air a televised version of the novel on its popular program *Playhouse 90* in September 1959. Unfortunately, the timing coincided with the state visit of Soviet premier Nikita Khrushchev, who had arrived for a twelve-day tour of the United States, prompting CBS to pull the show, which didn't air until April 1960.

Most Mount Dorans were getting an overdose of nuclear anxiety, whether they watched *Playhouse 90*, read Frank's novel or simply picked up a newspaper. Locally, many new homes were being built with bomb shelters, while existing homes were being retrofitted to provide safe places to sit out a nuclear blast. The most extraordinary revelation of the era's deeply embedded fear is the story of the Mount Dora Catacombs, the largest privately constructed nuclear fallout shelter in the nation.

* *The book's title is derived from Revelation 18:10: "Alas, alas, that great city Babylon, that mighty city! for in one hour is thy judgment come."*

For years, many considered tales of this multi-family sanctuary to be an urban legend, as the tight circle of people aware of its existence had been sworn to secrecy.

Initiated by Lake County health director Dr. James Hall, citrus magnate William Baker and businessman Theodore Mittendorf, the idea was for twenty-five families to pitch in nearly $2,000 each to have local builder J.G. Ray design and build the Catacombs. To disguise the purpose of the project and explain away the noise and excavation equipment shaking up the residential neighborhood, participants concocted a cover story that a tennis court was being installed. In reality, it was an oversized subterranean sanctuary capable of keeping one hundred people alive for at least six months. Those in on the secret would go underground, where food supplies were stashed, ten thousand rounds of ammunition and weapons were stored and jars containing seeds were ready for the day food could be grown again.

Fortunately, the bombs never dropped, and the families never went underground. But somewhere in Mount Dora there still exists the remains of an underground state-of-the-art fallout shelter dressed out with its own clinic, kitchen, showers, restrooms and recreation room.

The 1960s couldn't come soon enough.

Chapter 12

THE TIMES THEY ARE A-CHANGIN'

I intend to safeguard my family in the event of nuclear war.
–Mount Dora resident

Crisis Mode

If Americans thought that the 1960s would diminish Cold War anxiety, they were sadly mistaken. In 1961, a concerned Mount Dora resident who anticipated the impending Armageddon distributed a report titled *Challenge and Response Mount Dora* to city council members and other municipal officials. In it, the author asserted that it was urgent that city leaders develop a plan to reestablish Mount Dora following an attack: "In the manner of an engineer, it is blunt but honest…I intend to safeguard my family in the event of nuclear war, but recognize that our best chance for longer-range post-fallout survival would be as an organized community—not in anarchy and confusion among a few remaining survivors."

Within a year, the plan highlighting the common fears of the age would appear prescient, as the Cuban Missile Crisis brought the nation to the brink of a nuclear war. As the USSR deployed ballistic missiles in Cuba, the clock began ticking. And when America's negotiations with Russia seemed to be at an impasse, from the highest levels of government to the quietest neighborhoods in America, people prepared for the worst.

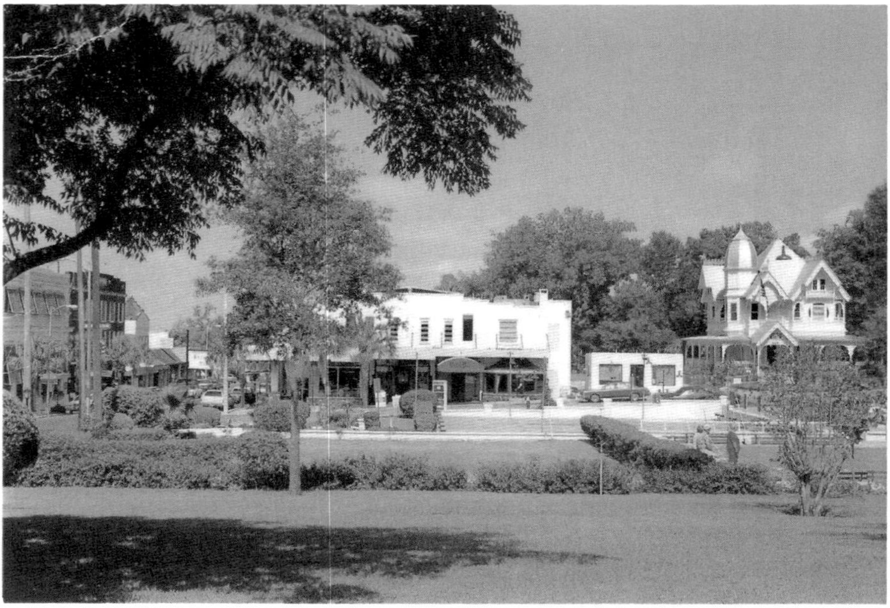

Annie Donnelly Park, with the 1893 Donnelly House on the right, in the 1960s. The peaceful image belies the widespread anxiety sparked by fears of a nuclear holocaust. *Mount Dora Historical Society.*

Anxieties in Mount Dora mirrored the nation's mood. On October 23, 1962, just one day after President Kennedy went on the air to address the nation about the stakes in this nuclear showdown, local residents were urged to attend a special city council meeting. When the meeting was called to order, city leaders and citizens discussed fallout shelters and public safety. In the event of war, they decided, the city would be divided into separate zones under the authority of individual defense captains. That night, each person holding a key position in city government was assigned an alternate to assume their responsibilities in the event they didn't survive.

Thankfully, through a combination of common sense, compromise and diplomacy between the nations, none of those scenarios came to pass. Within five days, the crisis de-escalated and the world began working its way back to normal. Across America, and in Mount Dora, it meant that citizens could once again look forward to the future. And if things changed, somewhere underground in Mount Dora there was still a bomb shelter that could accommodate one hundred people.

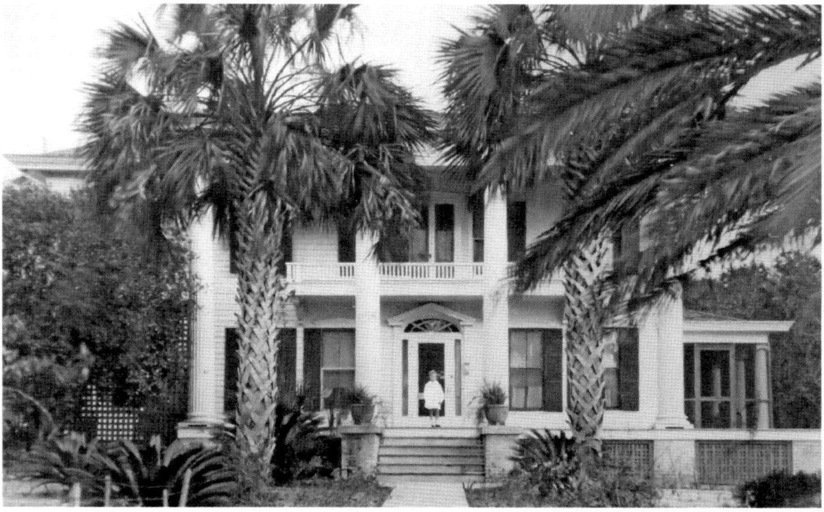

The historic Guller House, which once served as city hall, was moved and replaced by a newer city hall built in the same location. *Mount Dora Historical Society.*

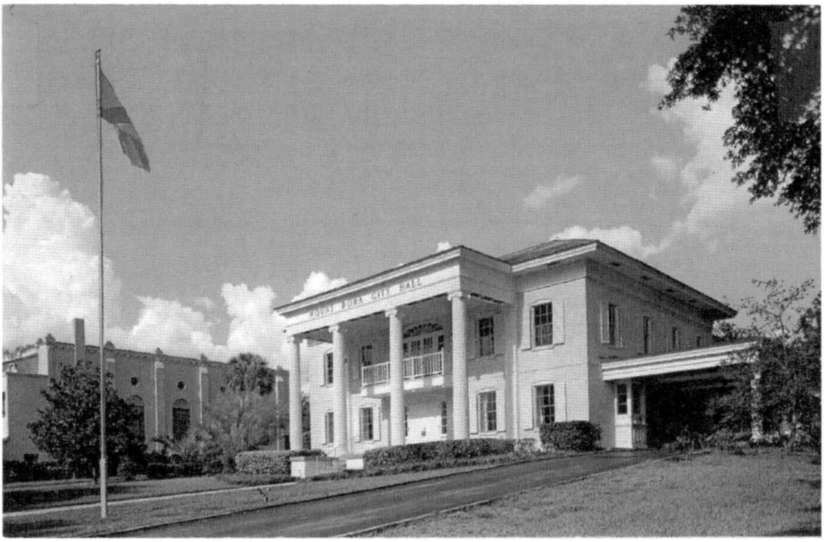

Inspired by the look of the Guller House, architect Brandon Wald copied its southern plantation style in the design of the renovated city hall that opened in 1964. *Mount Dora Historical Society.*

Get Outta Town

Even before the threat of nuclear was behind them, the city examined ways to enhance the quality of life. An obvious choice was attracting a school of higher education. The chance came in 1961 when the Florida legislature approved the creation of a junior college in Lake County. Eager city leaders sought to secure the school for Mount Dora by offering a forty-eight-acre parcel near Unser Street and Lincoln Avenue perfectly suited for a college campus. Although Mount Dora could've been a contender, the City of Leesburg promised to pony up seventy acres and secured the school. Regardless of the loss, Mount Dora continued to move forward. In the same year, a new post office opened its doors at Donnelly and

Madam President

The social and cultural changes taking place across America in the '60s arrived in Mount Dora in 1961. That's when Margaret Lofroos, the daughter of Bob White, became the first female president of city council. Perhaps a small step in the scheme of things, it seemed to be a major leap in conservative Mount Dora.

On her first night as president, Lofroos was considered a success by relieved citizens as well as members of the media when she managed to whittle down the usual four-hour marathon meetings into productive and efficient sessions.

In just ninety minutes, the newly elected president corralled the council to review an engineering report on a water improvement program; authorized bids for a new police car; condemned a home; approved a bid to paint the fire station, Lawn Bowling Club and Community Building; opened discussion on natural gas distribution; and made committee assignments.

Onlookers were impressed. "Under her suggestion," wrote the *Mount Dora Topic*, "the city fathers agreed to a new meeting procedure designed to speed up official business and, of all things, cut down on rambling speech making."

In January 1978, Margaret Lofroos was sworn in as the city's first female mayor.

Seventh Avenue, and a new Presbyterian church greeted parishioners at McDonald and Sixth Avenue. The most anticipated arrival in years, the Golden Triangle Shopping Center, appeared north of Sylvan Shores, ushering shoppers into the future of retail: strip malls. But with it came the unexpected side effect of ushering shoppers out of downtown. Compared with the modern new plaza, stores in the downtown district began to look tired and dingy. With the new highway routing potential customers far outside the city center, sales began to slump. By mid-1964, a dozen business owners had moved out of downtown, leaving vacant storefronts in their wake.

Now the challenge of boosting downtown became crucial. Business owners and landlords met to discuss ways of luring customers back. Searching for new ideas, they carpooled to Winter Park, where independent merchants had created an active, upscale park-like shopping village along Park Avenue. With this as their inspiration, they developed a multi-phase plan. In addition to a new catchphrase ("A Touch of New England"), Phase I was a face-lift, and by chance, the timing was right to obtain some of the raw materials they needed. To make room for a parking lot at Fourth Avenue and Alexander Street, the historic Crane House had been demolished. From the rubble, piles of bricks were plucked, cleaned and recycled for use as storefront accents and decorative planter boxes.

Another part of the plan was soliciting input from the community. A public contest invited residents to propose ideas for rejuvenating downtown. In her fifty-dollar prize-winning proposal, Dorothy Crone offered the idea of a "downtown council" that would issue a calendar of events, operate a downtown visitors center and host "Mount Dora Days"—an event that would include "exhibits, activities, displays, and special sales that will exploit our city of happy living."

To expand on the concept, an enterprising resident recalled the popularity of S&H Green Stamps and suggested that they print sheets of "Mount Dora Trading Stamps." In short order, more than two dozen area businesses were distributing the stamps to eager shoppers. By the time the program concluded, more than 1,875 fully completed books had been exchanged for free merchandise.

This truly was a city of happy living.

Condo, Condo, Condo

Mount Dora was approaching the end of its first century when residents pondered where the city should go next. At an April 19, 1965 public meeting, city planners, officials and interested citizens concluded that preserving Mount Dora's small-town charm was paramount, yet there was also a sense that the town needed to enter the modern age.

Slowly, gradually, historic homes were replaced by contemporary architecture. In the latter half of the 1960s, the First National Bank built a modern headquarters directly across from the new post office. Several years later, J.P. Donnelly's circa 1887 Bishopgate, which sat behind the post office, was bulldozed to make room for the bank's parking lot. Today, only a carriage steppingstone is left as a reminder of what had been. Nearby, the historic Villa Dora hotel was razed and replaced by a towering six-story condominium, and on the north side of Donnelly Park, developers erected a new low-rise condominium.

Changes quickened in the 1970s, with two of Mount Dora's most recognizable landmarks reaching their final days. In the downtown shopping village, the Princess Theatre faded to black when audiences grew tired of watching B-movies in a neglected theater. After its doors closed, its contents were shipped to a theater in Honduras, and an Arabian-themed discotheque called 1,001 Nights moved in for a brief run.

More growth was on the way. In 1972, E. Everett Huskey, one of Orlando's leading developers, decided that Mount Dora was worth an

How to Succeed in Business

In 1973, the Mount Dora Area Chamber of Commerce moved into the former Atlantic Coast Line Railroad depot, where it continued a mission that began in the 1920s. Then, as now, the chamber welcomed guests from across America and around the world, acquainting them with Mount Dora's activities, dining, lodging, neighborhoods, retailers, civic groups and, in particular, its affiliated businesses and services. As the "front door" to the town, the chamber is traditionally the first stop for visitors, future residents and business owners.

www.mountdora.com

investment. Opening an office in the old home of the First National Bank at Fifth and Donnelly, he announced plans for a $1.2 million condominium complex at the southern entrance to town. It was approved. He later informed the city he planned to add ten stories to his downtown office to create "Huskey Tower." That was denied. In fact, things were happening too quickly. Several other condo projects that depended on the demolition of historic homes had been proposed and approved before a council member suggested a moratorium on multi-family housing units. The motion passed unanimously.

There were other signs that historic preservation was becoming part of the community's consciousness. Two years after the chamber of commerce recycled the old Seaboard Coast Line railroad depot to make it its headquarters. Then, in 1975, the historic Donnelly House, owned and occupied by Lodge No. 238 of the Fraternal and Accepted Masons, was named to the National Register of Historic Places.

As Mount Dora's first century was coming to a close, in 1978 James Simpson celebrated his 100th birthday. The first white child born in Mount Dora could look around and see that in his lifetime his hometown had

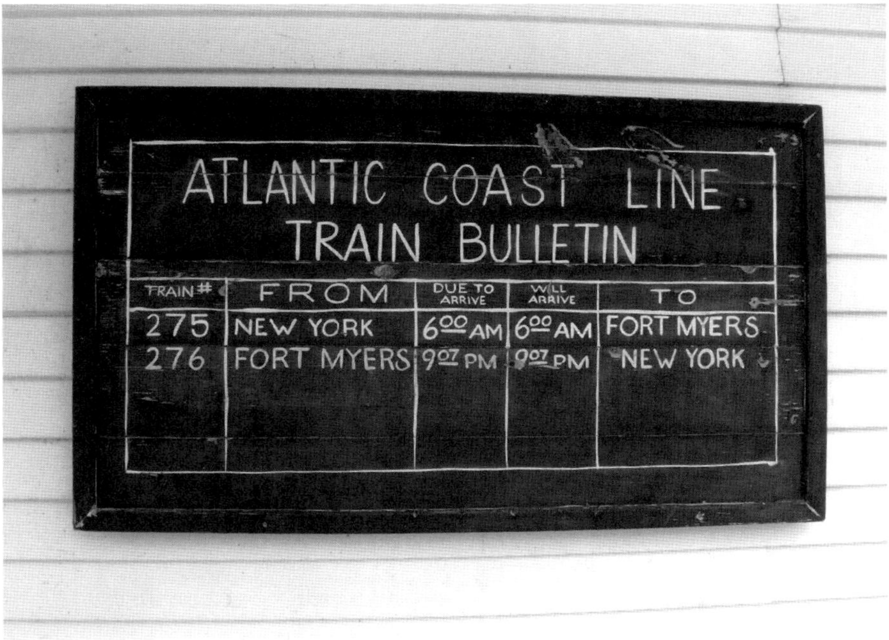

Although tourist trains still pick up passengers, the scheduled arrivals are only memories on a sign at the old depot. *Nancy Howell.*

changed from an empty wilderness into an active and diverse community. Mount Dora could provide nearly every luxury and convenience anyone could want without the nuisance of heavy traffic, noise and congestion.

By the end of the 1970s, Mount Dora had reached an enviable position. It was attracting people who didn't *need* to live here but *chose* to live here.

Flashback to 1975: You Gotta Have Art

Sponsored by the Mount Dora Center for the Arts, the Mount Dora Arts Festival was launched in 1975 as a one-time event. Drawing an estimated 50,000 people, its initial success led to its return as an annual event. While the Center for the Arts maintains a full calendar of programs, classes, exhibitions, art openings and fine art auction, the organization's annual two-day juried Arts Festival remains its signature event, with nearly 300 artists displaying oil paintings, watercolors, acrylics, clay, sculpture, photography, jewelry and more. The popular event attracts an incredible 300,000 visitors to Mount Dora the first weekend in February.

www.mountdoracenterforthearts.org

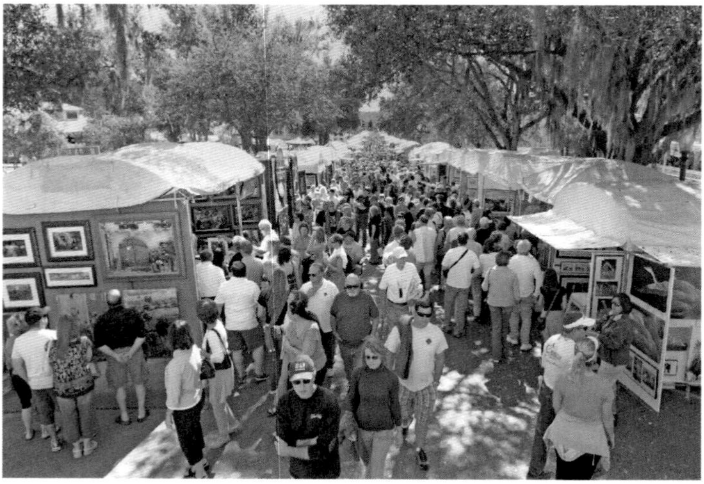

Each February, the Mount Dora Art Festival attracts hundreds of thousands of visitors, who admire the works of nearly three hundred artists. *Mount Dora Center for the Arts.*

Chapter 13
GETTING BETTER ALL THE TIME

A pointless exercise excessive in its unrelenting vulgarity.
—Wall Street Journal

Two Thumbs Down

Between 1980 and 2000, Mount Dora underwent a period of significant change. At the beginning of the 1980s, major events such as the Arts Festival and Bicycle Festival were hitting their stride, and when the Craft Fair joined the lineup and other events filled in the calendar, Mount Dora could justify its self-appointed title "Festival City."

And there was something else happening in Mount Dora: *movies.* To be fair, it was just one movie. And to be really fair, that one movie happened to be *Honky Tonk Freeway*, a film that remains a point of pride and/or embarrassment for many locals. Released in 1981, the movie turned Mount Dora into the fictional town of Ticlaw, which needed a highway exit to attract visitors (reflecting, perhaps coincidentally, the freeway that bypassed downtown). The $25 million film directed by John Schlesinger (*Midnight Cowboy*, *Marathon Man*) featured some of Hollywood's finest: Jessica Tandy, Hume Cronyn, Teri Garr, Beau Bridges, Beverly D'Angelo, Daniel Stern, William Devane, David Rasche and Howard Hesseman.

At a time when motion picture production was a rarity in central Florida, the selection of Mount Dora as the setting for *Honky Tonk Freeway* was a major event. A casting call went out, and about two thousand extras from

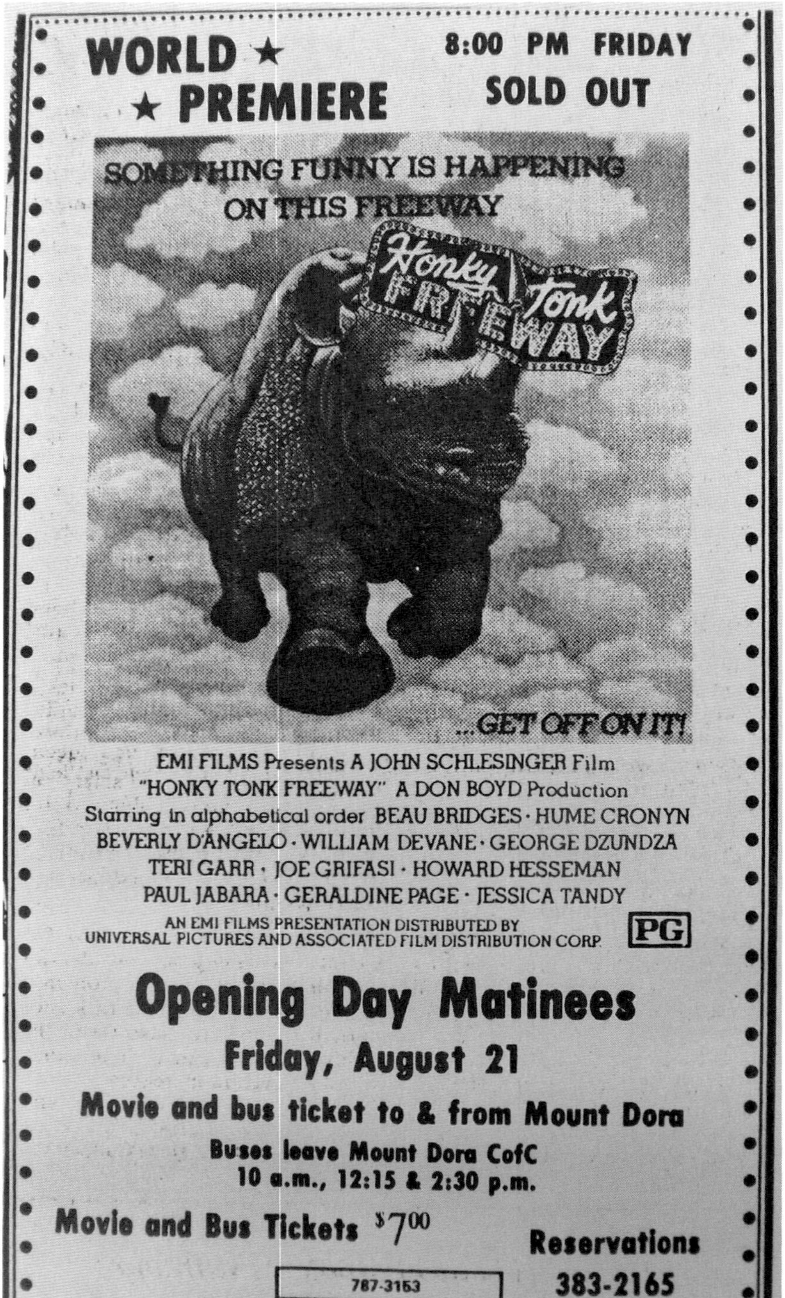

Although the making of a major motion picture in town sounded like a good idea, many residents were livid following the premiere of *Honky Tonk Freeway*. *Mount Dora Historical Society.*

near and far arrived to earn $35 per day for the privilege of being in a real talking picture. Downtown merchants fared better. They received $100 each day that shooting disrupted their business.

Among the integral scenes dictated by the script were two that would become embedded in local history. First, parts of the shopping village would be painted pink, and second, an elephant named Bubbles would step onto enormous water skis and be towed around Lake Dora. But that wasn't all.

The film, which marked novice screenwriter Edward Clinton's first and only feature effort, suffered from a weak script, poor marketing and a limited release of a single week. Its fate was sealed. Wikipedia profiles it as "one of the most expensive box office flops in history," one that lost "its British backers Thorn-EMI an estimated $11 million, profoundly impacting its fortunes and aspirations." Following the film's release, *Time* magazine asked rhetorically, "What can you get for $25 million these days?" The *Wall Street Journal* observed, "*Honky Tonk Freeway* is a pointless exercise excessive in its unrelenting vulgarity." Expressing a gentler tone, the *Dallas Morning News* called it "a pile up. A calamity."

Things really hit the fan when locals got a chance to see it. After attending the film's gala premiere at Leesburg's Tropic Theatre, many vented their frustrations. "Mount Dora's moral and cultural standard has surely been dragged through the muck with the showing of the film *Honky Tonk Freeway*," began one letter to the editor. "I feel the least that our city council and chamber of commerce could do would be to publish a letter of apology to the residents (for) consenting to have parts of it filmed here."

Another resident added, "Those of us who squirmed through its showing were witness to the demeaning of America in a completely spastic presentation of something to offend everyone." Another took exception with, well, *everything*. "Not only as an American, but also as a resident of Mount Dora, do I resent this movie. Our town has surely been sold out for a few pieces of silver and I, too, feel betrayed. Have we lost our collective minds!"

Over time, an inexplicable fondness for the flop has replaced the palpable disgust that arose during the film's premiere. Today, many residents have learned to laugh about it; some even take a peculiar pride in the movie. In a few gift and antique shops, you can still find rare pieces of *Honky Tonk Freeway* memorabilia, items that preserve forever the time when Mount Dora's shopping village was painted pink and an elephant named Bubbles skied across Lake Dora.

A Beautiful Day in the Neighborhood

The unfulfilled promise of *Honky Tonk Freeway* aside, it was through festivals and events that tens of thousands of visitors first saw Mount Dora and discovered its charm. Some would visit for a few hours or a weekend, but as more and more visitors began recalling memories of the past while strolling the quaint village and picturesque neighborhoods, many decided to make Mount Dora home. They became either seasonal or permanent residents, often buying and renovating vintage homes, becoming active in community events and participating on committees. Some commuted to work in Orlando, Winter Park, Altamonte Springs, Sanford and across the metropolitan area, while others pursued their dream by launching their own local business. Many newcomers were content with the town as they found it, while a few would try to turn Mount Dora into the place they left behind. Although many eager residents would pitch hundreds of ideas to improve the community over the years, the vast majority were dismissed by locals who preferred to keep things just the way they were.

This was the beginning of Mount Dora's transformation from a sleepy southern town into a desirable destination. But still, there were challenges. Even though Mount Dora had the look, it didn't have the business. That was about to change.

Flashback to 1984: Good at Their Crafts

Following the success of the February Arts Festival and October Bicycle Festival, which were welcoming thousands of people, members of the Downtown Merchants Association looked for an opening. They decided that Mount Dora needed a craft fair. Since its premiere in 1984, the nationally ranked juried event now attracts about 200,000 visitors annually. Filling the main and side streets of the village on the third weekend of October, about 400 of the nation's best crafters display pottery, paintings, wood carvings, jewelry, art glass, paper, fabrics, soaps and many other handcrafted items.

www.mountdoracraftfair.com

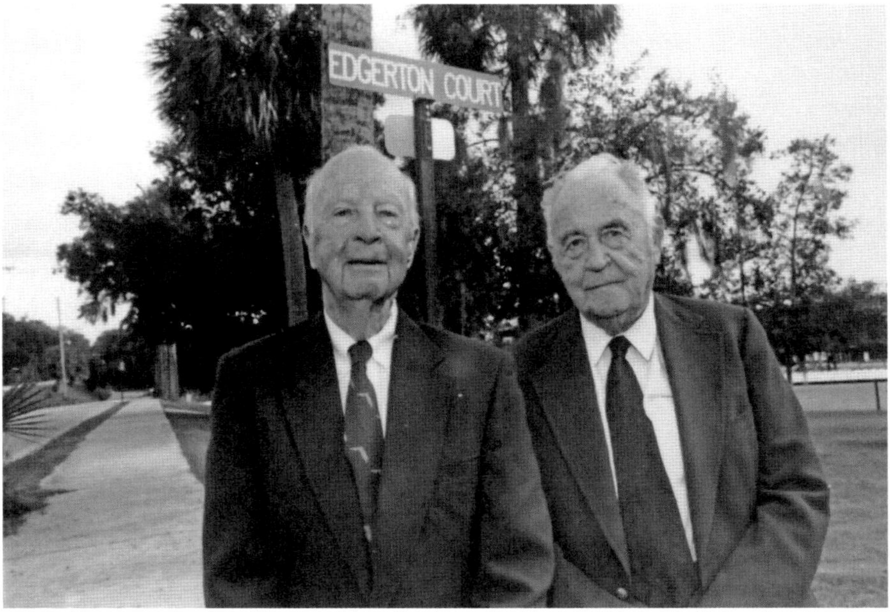

Brothers Richard and David Edgerton. Richard, who ran the Lakeside Inn for several decades, was instrumental in getting the highway routed around town, which David wrote about in his book on Mount Dora's history. *Mount Dora Historical Society.*

The Renaissance

For first-time visitors, the vintage buildings and storefronts evoked a sense of nostalgia, as though the city were frozen in the 1950s. In a sense, *it was.*

Longtime residents could tell you that the Mount Dora of the '80s and '90s owed a debt of gratitude to an earlier generation. As a result of Governor LeRoy Collins, Richard Edgerton* and other supportive residents working to route the new highway around the town, the urban sprawl of strip malls, chain stores and fast-food restaurants had been relegated to the busy four-lane highway a mile away. The buffer zone created by the new highway had placed downtown in a kind of suspended animation for nearly three decades. Although locals could still walk to the village and find a few stores, for the most part, retailers were still scarce.

**Richard Edgerton passed on in 2001, insisting that he never knew exactly what transpired following his call to the governor, but he spoke modestly on the need to take action at the time and then gave credit where credit was due. "It would have split the town in two," he said. "It was a situation that came along and we took care of it…Actually, the* governor *took care of it."*

Things started to change, ever so slowly, around 1987. Rents were still affordable, and mom and pop shops were still possible. Helping nudge things forward were New Yorkers Vince Calvo and Jim Anderson. Smitten by the appearance of the village and impressed by Renee Milota, an energetic downtown merchant, Calvo and Anderson purchased a home and a building, and after testing a restaurant and shoe store and lingerie shop, they settled on an upscale boutique. Gay New Yorkers opening a fashionable dress shop in Mount Dora clearly signaled a new direction. And more changes would follow.

When other businesses would close by early afternoon, Calvo kept Yesterday, Today & Tomorrow open late. And when downtown went into hibernation on Sundays, Calvo decided that if he wasn't making money six days a week, he might as well not make money seven days a week and began opening his doors on Sunday. For months, this new approach to retail was all a matter of faith, until locals and visitors began taking notice that Mount Dora was turning a corner. As word about this up-and-coming village got out, the dry cleaners, jewelry stores, sandwich shop and bus station became neighbors with art galleries, sidewalk cafés, antique shops, upscale restaurants and independent bookshops. One of the most visible improvements came when realtor Lucy Hummell showed Buddy and Valerie Hart the long-abandoned Mount Dora Hotel. While some

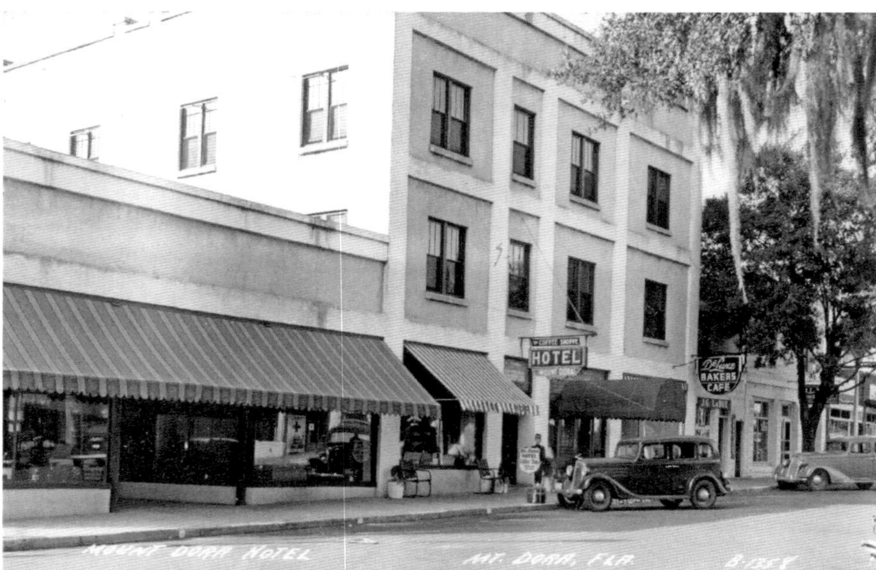

The Mount Dora Hotel was central to downtown. After a long period of decline, Buddy and Valerie Hart saved the building in the early 1990s and converted it into a collection of shops, restaurants and offices. *Mount Dora Historical Society.*

thought that the derelict building, which sat squarely in the middle of Mount Dora's most sought-after retail space, should be razed to make room for a parking lot, the Miami couple had a better idea. They bought the multistoried building and renovated it into a collection of shops, restaurants and offices. It was aptly named the Renaissance.

All of this new activity was surrounded by neighborhoods of historic homes, white picket fences, oak trees and Spanish moss, an expansive lakefront and the sweet perfume of orange blossoms. Soon magazines and newspapers, including *AAA World*, *Southern Living* and *Florida Travel & Life*, began to profile the town in glowing feature articles; many more publications would follow their lead, including *Money* magazine, which in 1994 named Mount Dora the third-best place to retire in America (or, as some pointed out, the *first*-best place in Florida).

Just as the pioneers realized a century earlier, individuals could put their stamp on the future by dreaming of a better world…and then building it.

Many Hands Make Light Work

During this period, citizens were also building a new look for Lake Dora's waterfront. Recognizing the lack of a sidewalk along the shoreline, Billy Osborne became the citizen champion of what would become one of the most recognized and well-loved landmarks in town. He contacted Jim Snell, director of public works, to suggest a walkway that would connect Palm Island to the downtown district. In turn, Snell recruited Judy Smathers in the Recreation Department and Bob Shultz of the Parks Department and launched a public-private initiative that would beautify the shoreline and lead to one of the city's most photographed landmarks.

Following months of meetings and discussions, the city determined that if the citizens could raise donations for Lighthouse Walk, it would provide the labor. In January 1989, Osborne created the Mount Dora Civic Enhancement Association, and within five months, donations had arrived from citizens, banks, homeowners associations, civic groups, businesses, service organizations and the chamber of commerce. Donors contributing $500 or more were promised a bronze plaque.

Ultimately, the six-foot-wide pathway tied together several community landmarks: the Palm Island Boardwalk, Gilbert Park, Grantham Point, the marina and the Lawn Bowling Club. Topping off the project, designers added a special touch at the end of Grantham Point: a fully-functioning lighthouse.

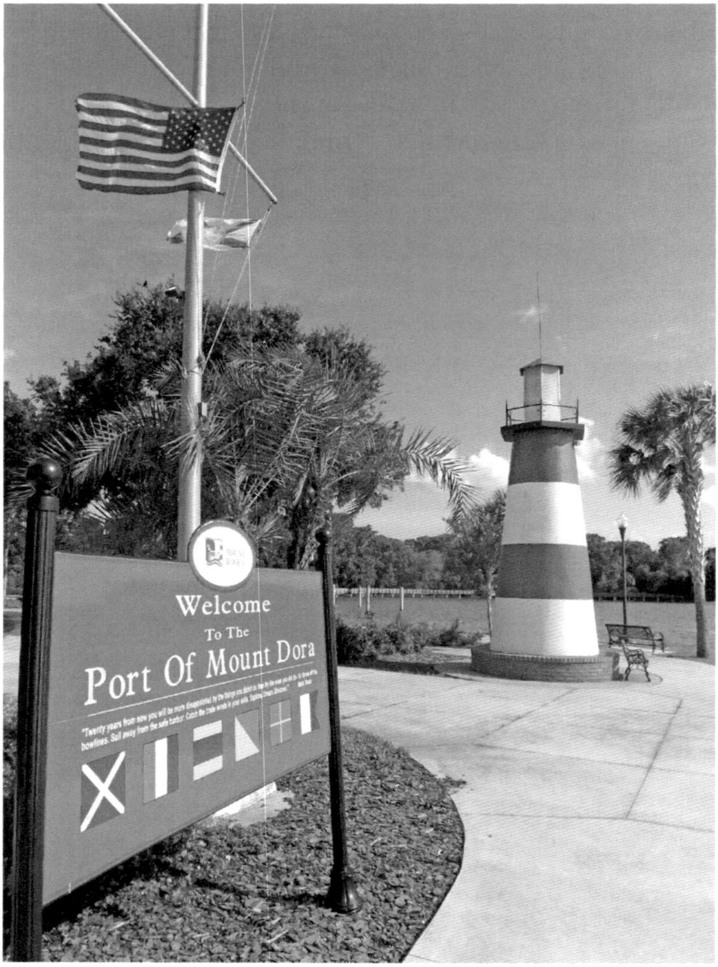

A Coast Guard–certified inland lighthouse is the highlight at the active port of Mount Dora. *Nancy Howell.*

According to Bonnie Rourke of *Lighthouse Digest* magazine, the idea of a lighthouse was sparked when Jim Snell overheard a fisherman explaining that in the dark he could only navigate the lake by following the shoreline. A light went off for Snell, who thought that a lighthouse near the boat launch would help all boaters.

Donations for this phase of the project arrived, resulting in a thirty-five-foot-tall $3,000 beacon of brick and stucco. While it merely looks like a decorative accent piece, it is in fact the only registered inland freshwater lighthouse in Florida, using a 750-watt pulsator to guide

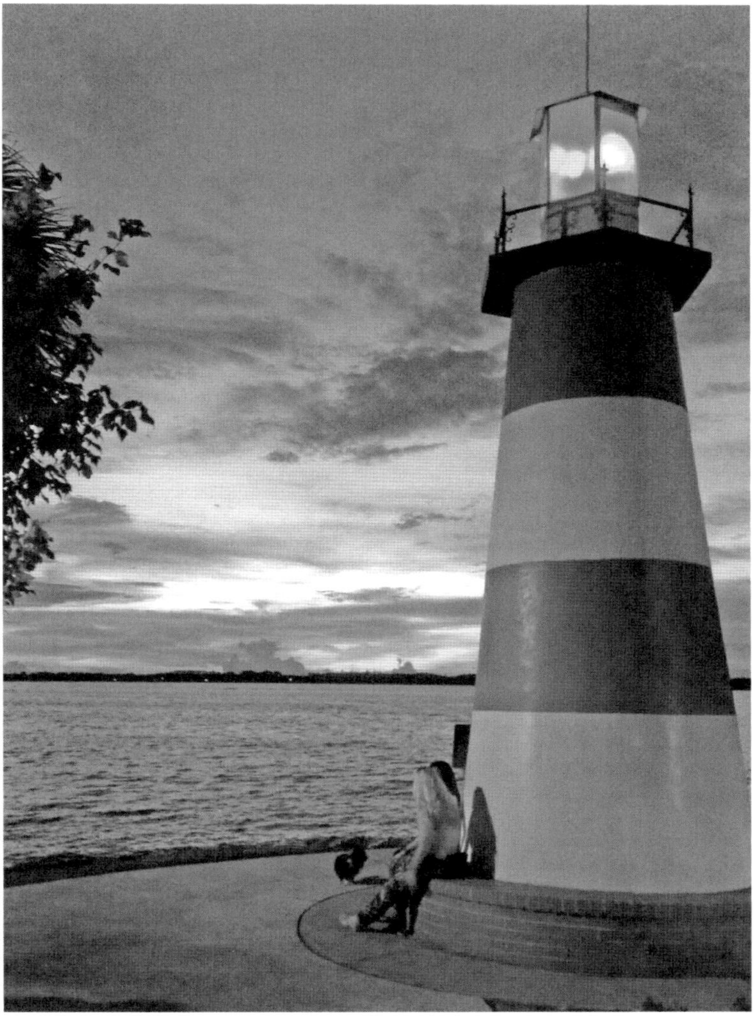

The lighthouse at Grantham Point is a popular gathering place throughout the day and especially in the evening at sunset. *Nancy Howell.*

boaters across Lake Dora. It quickly became a point of pride for the city, the chamber and merchants who incorporated its image on just about anything from logos, maps and promotional brochures to letterhead, websites and assorted souvenirs.

More importantly, the lighthouse became a gathering place. To this day, locals and visitors walk to the lighthouse to reflect on the beauty of Lake Dora and savor radiant sunsets. Each day since its dedication, the lighthouse has done what it was designed to do: bring people home.

Stormy Weather

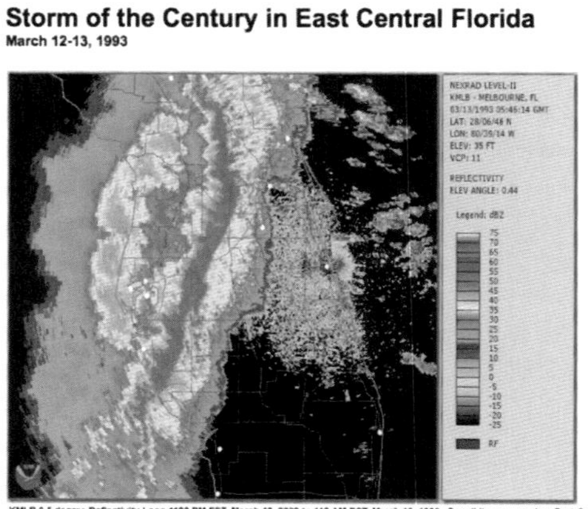

A satellite image shows the squall line of the "Storm of the Century," which clobbered Mount Dora on March 13, 1993, leading to the loss of lives, homes and hundreds of oak trees. *noaa.gov.*

Perhaps the most devastating weather event since the Great Freeze of 1894–95 was the "Storm of the Century," which slammed Mount Dora on the evening of March 13, 1993.

After slicing up Florida's southwest coast, the storm barreled over central Florida, whipping up tornadoes that skipped over Lake Dora and into nearby neighborhoods. Wind gusts ripped off awnings and shingles from homes and businesses and caused aging oak trees that once formed canopied roads to collapse. Of forty-four Florida deaths attributed to the storm, three were in Mount Dora.

There was hardly a neighborhood untouched by the storm. More than a dozen homes were destroyed, nearly 250 homes were damaged and power was cut off to many residents, who endured a prolonged cold snap that followed in the storm's wake.

The morning after, as the winds were subsiding, residents assessed the damage. Soon after, they took chain saws to broken tree limbs, swept up towering mounds of debris, covered rooftops with tarps and got back to business. Indicative of the spirit of the town, a scheduled St. Patrick's Day celebration took on a new twist at the Lakeside Inn. With emergency generators working overtime, coolers filled with corned beef and kegs of green beer, management decided that it would treat storm-weary residents to a community party where the cover charge was a single roof shingle (which could be found by the thousands across town).

Recovering from the storm, the 1990s found Mount Dora easing into its new role as a destination. Merchants were prospering, homes were being renovated and festivals were getting bigger. Considering Mount Dora's history, in a 1993 interview one resident placed the credit where it was due. "One hundred years ago this was a vacation destination," said Sonny Rehbaum, owner of Rehbaum's Hardware. "By the 1900s, civic-minded people were planting oak trees and installing streetlights and making investments for the future which we take for granted today. We don't even know who they were or some of the things these people did out of the love for their community—but Mount Dora is the result of many, many, many people."

Chapter 14

MOUNT DORA TODAY

When Mount Dora entered the twenty-first century, it was with a drive that would elevate the town far beyond what the early settlers could have ever envisioned. The city was in the mood for renovation. There would be large plans and impressive results. Donnelly Park received a makeover with an expanded pavilion and outdoor stage, as well as new courts for tennis and pickleball. A multi-phase makeover of downtown added an improved look with wider sidewalks, a pedestrian walk, updated and newly painted storefronts and new informational signage. Some beloved oaks were uprooted in favor of palms, which sparked an outburst of protests. Floating docks were added at Grantham Point, with a three-acre dog park quickly becoming a gathering spot for people with pets, and the circa 1929 Community Building was modernized to regain its role as the city's premier venue. The library underwent an expansion as the dedicated staff pushed operations into high gear with movies, guest speakers, special programs and book sales. Even the chamber of commerce was making major improvements to its home in the old railroad depot. Outside the chamber's doors, the city revamped Childs Park into Sunset Park, a new outdoor venue.

When attendance at the Arts Festival and Craft Fair reached record numbers, one fringe benefit was introducing hundreds of thousands of visitors to the town, as well as a calendar full of festivals, concerts and holiday events.

In the village, entrepreneurs opened bakeries and delis, candy and cupcake shops, ice cream parlors, coffee and wine bars, day spas and salons, bookstores, gift shops and a modernism museum. There are places to buy

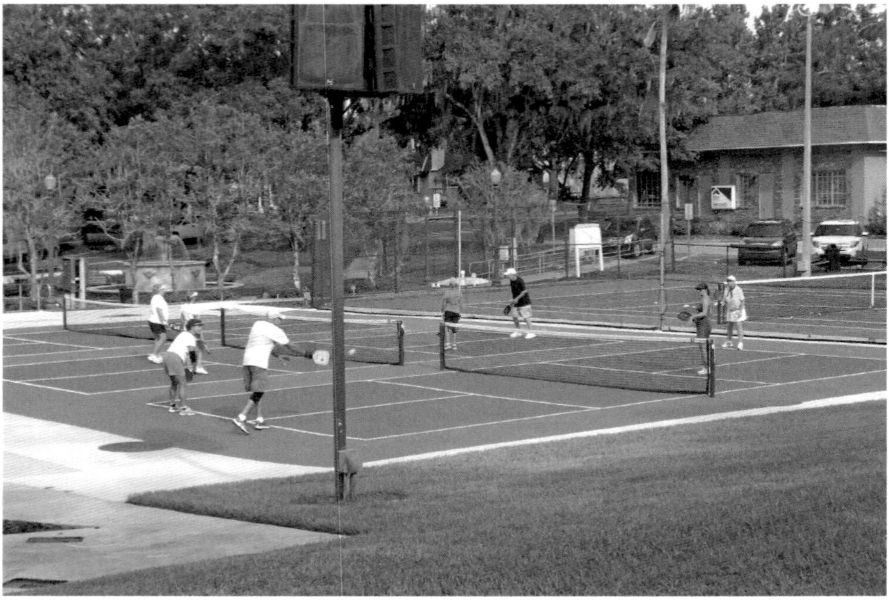

Sold to the city by J.P. Donnelly and named for his late wife, Annie, Donnelly Park has been the town's gathering place for concerts, tennis, pickleball, movies and special events like the holiday Light Up celebration. *Nancy Howell.*

cigars, souvenirs, olive oil, guns, clocks, kitchenware, books, pottery, crafts, clothing, footwear, jewelry, antiques and even freshly baked biscuits for your pet. And Mount Dora has become a veritable United Nations of dining with menus covering Cuban, Mexican, French, Thai, British, German, Peruvian and Italian meals, as well as good ol' American fare. In 2015, another first occurred when celebrity chef Norman Van Aken announced the opening of a new restaurant on Fourth Avenue.

Along the southern entrance to town, Community Redevelopment Agency renovations helped develop the "Uptown Mount Dora" retail district along Highland Avenue, attracting gutsy merchants eager to capitalize on lower rents and increased opportunities. The more bohemian atmosphere proved to be a good fit for antique malls, casual restaurants, microbreweries and even a car museum and a New Age shop that decided to place their bets on the future of uptown Mount Dora.

On the flip side, in the 1960s, when a dozen vacancies alarmed village merchants, they took action to revitalize the shopping village. In contrast, for reasons unknown and unaddressed, a landlord's prime commercial properties—including entire blocks of the historic village—have remained dark and noticeably vacant for years.

PAYING IT FORWARD

In the millennium's first few years, the urge to become part of the community increased exponentially, and the demand for real estate followed suit. Those who ignored the lessons of Miami's boom and bust in the 1920s, though, would pay the price when the Great Recession of 2008 torpedoed the market.

Regardless, as neighboring Orlando and distant south Florida became overpopulated pressure cookers, many viewed Mount Dora as a safety valve. There was something different about this town where neighborhoods of bungalows and cottages and turn-of-the-century homes looked much the same as they had since they were first created. The highway that encircled Mount Dora like a force field continued to protect it. Outside the circle, though, forests began to disappear like funeral pyres, and when the smoke cleared, new subdivisions and planned communities sprang up. Elaborate signs often using "Mount" or "Dora" or "Lake" (and sometimes a combination of the three) implied proximity to and association with the town. The likelihood

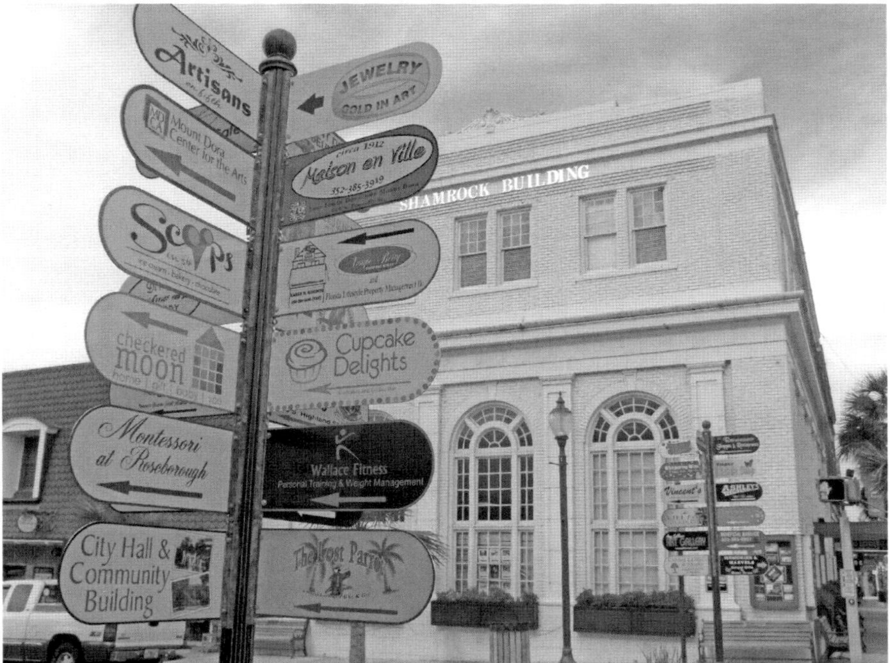

Several phases of redevelopment—including improved signage, sidewalks and parking in the historic shopping village—were completed in 2015. Several much-loved oak trees, however, gave way to palms. *Nancy Howell.*

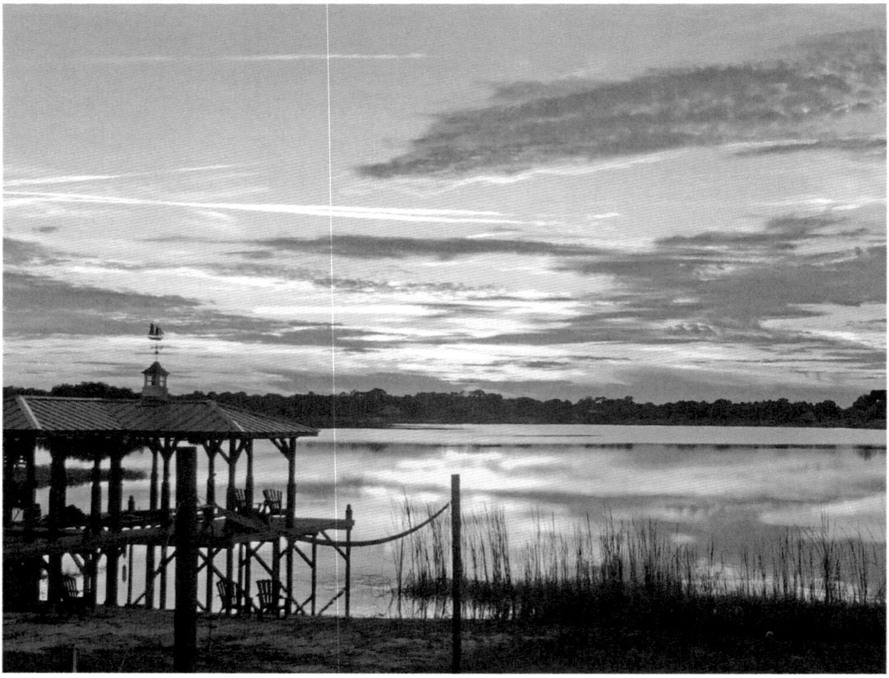

A sunset over Lake Gertrude evokes memories of Old Florida. *Nancy Howell.*

that additional subdivisions will arrive is a near certainty as the Wekiva Parkway, the last link in an expressway encircling Greater Orlando, nears completion with an extension leading to the entrance of Mount Dora.

Ultimately, it doesn't matter whether you live in a gated subdivision, on a lake, in East Town or even the historic district. Mount Dora is not just a single neighborhood—it is a community in every sense of the word. And what exists today is the collective result of generations of people who took an active role in creating this place we call home.

Inherited from the past, its future has been placed in the hands of concerned citizens and elected officials who, voters trust, will put their self-interests aside. The story of Mount Dora is being created by community-minded citizens who participate in clubs and organizations; who join committees and volunteer their time; and who produce events, organize activities and give back for the sake of giving.

It continues with police officers who patrol the streets, firefighters who respond to emergencies and merchants and restaurateurs who were bold enough to bet on themselves and their businesses. The essence of Mount Dora is also in the amateur actors who entertain, the students and teachers who work with (and for) the benefit of one another in public and private schools and the citizens who protest vigorously when something threatens the well-being of this community and work tirelessly to keep the town on the right path.

While this brief history begins more than a century and a half ago, it should always be a source of pride knowing that the torch passed on by the founding families has been handled with care by successive generations. Everyone who calls Mount Dora home owes a debt of gratitude to their predecessors, as well as a responsibility to do their level best to honor our past and improve the community for the future.

Chapter 15

MOUNT DORA

The More You Know

PRESERVING THE PAST

Keeping track of the town's past has been the passion of the Mount Dora Historical Society, which grew out of the Mount Dora Tourist Club and was formed in conjunction with the research and release of R.J. Longstreet's *The Story of Mount Dora, Florida* in 1960.

Over the years, there has been consistent interest in defining and sharing the story of Mount Dora. One role of the society is preserving items from the past, including photographs, letters, documents, oral

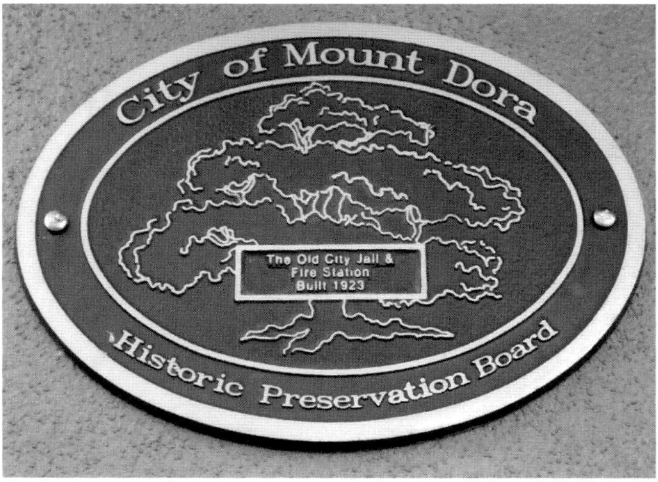

Found on homes and buildings of historic significance, markers like these are approved by the Historic Preservation Board. This denotes the Old City Jail and Fire Station, now home of the Mount Dora History Museum. *Nancy Howell.*

histories, heirlooms and even a house. Under the leadership of Dave Felts, in 1992 the historical society arranged to pick up and move a two-story 1905 farmhouse located downtown to a prominent location several blocks north on Donnelly Street. The former home of Charles and Alfida Simpson was restored, and the renamed Unity House served as the headquarters of the historical society for several years. Years later, the city took ownership of the house and renamed it the Simpson Farm House and Meeting Center.

The face of the historical society is the Mount Dora History Museum, housed in the town's first fire station and jail. Inside, displays tell the story of early railroads, mail delivery, the citrus industry, churches, Chautauqua, lodging and other highlights from the city's past.

www.mountdorahistorymuseum.com

Chautauqua: The Sequel

Even after the former Chautauqua grounds became the foundation of Heim's Sylvan Shores, the people of Mount Dora could never forget how those social and educational events had advanced the town's development. While Chautauqua's overwhelming appeal of the 1880s could not be duplicated, abbreviated versions of the social, cultural and spiritual events were staged in Mount Dora throughout the 1920s. In 1926, locals contacted the Washington, D.C.–based Radcliffe Chautauqua and arranged a three-day gathering featuring "Three Eloquent Speakers," including C.M. Eichelberger, who was later named vice-president of the United Nations Association. A variety show of musical acts was also on the bill, including Miss Lelia Lowry ("One of Chautauqua's Most Brilliant Accordionists") and Franz Gerl's Swiss Alpine Singers and Yodelers. And all for just two dollars!

A Walk in the Woods

To get a glimpse of the wilderness as seen by the earliest settlers, stroll along Palm Island Park. Located adjacent to Grantham Point, the eight-acre park on the shores of Lake Dora is easy to explore. In 2013, a $1.2 million renovation and expansion of a boardwalk was completed so nature lovers can take in images of Mount Dora from another perspective. The boardwalk skirts the waterfront, and pathways dip into the woods. Along the way, you may see alligators skimming beneath the surface, egrets perching on cypress branches and bald eagles searching for a fish dinner. Peaceful and serene, it's a largely undisturbed setting where you can enjoy cool lake breezes and the sights and sounds of nature.

www.floridahikes.com/palmislandpark

The W.T. Bland Public Library: The Gift that Keeps on Giving

Reflecting Mount Dora's unquenchable thirst for knowledge is the popularity of the W.T. Bland Public Library. The seeds of today's library were planted in 1905, when Betsy Rodgers bequeathed 150 books that were then circulated from a single room in the town hall. By 1917, the collection had been moved to the Educational Hall, where you could check out books—provided you happened to drop in on one of the two afternoons the librarian was on duty (and you had paid your one-dollar annual fee).

Once operated by the Women's Club of Mount Dora, after the library became a city department in 1960, a second branch was opened at the former Milner-Rosenwald Academy. When the main branch outgrew its home, a new library was constructed in 1976 on the corner of Donnelly Street and Ninth Avenue.

Residents accustomed to a library that had more books than space weren't surprised when the new library moved once again in 1995. While the new fifteen-thousand-square-foot library more than doubled in size,

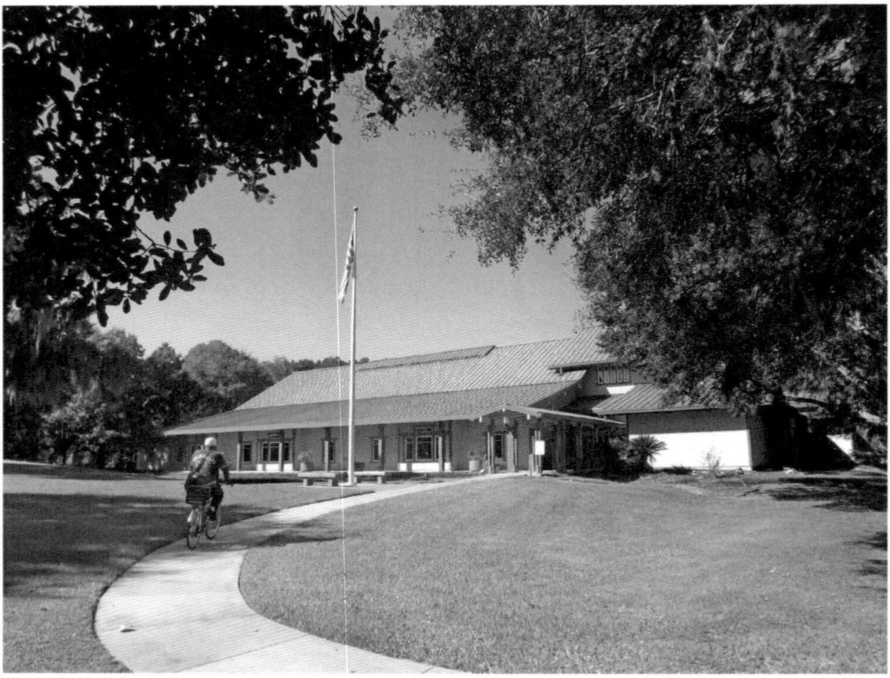

The W.T. Bland Public Library is one of the most active and engaging libraries in central Florida. In addition to offering books and videos, the dedicated staff organizes and hosts a wide range of popular classes and activities. *Nancy Howell.*

bookworms demanded more reading materials, leading to a six-thousand-square foot expansion completed in 2012.

As reported by David Cohea in the *Mount Dora Citizen*, as of 2015 the W.T. Bland Public Library had nearly 85,000 items in its holdings and access to hundreds of thousands more as part of the county-wide library system. There are roughly 9,000 e-books, 5,700 audio books and 11,500 DVDs. More than 12,000 patrons made more than 300,000 visits to the library in 2014, checking out more than 250,000 items, the majority being returned on time.

In recent years, the library staff and volunteers have created a service that is far more than the sum of its parts. Throughout the year, there are children's activities, movie nights, lectures, computer training and holiday events. The library even features a butterfly garden. Residents are given a helping hand through language courses, tax preparation and the use of computer workstations.

More than a library, it is a full-service learning environment—and one of the city's most valuable resources.

A Calendar of Events

Mount Dora became known as "Festival City" thanks to a full calendar of events and activities (for a complete listing, visit www.mountdora.com). Among the major festivals:

- January: Renninger's Antique Extravaganza, Highwaymen Art Show
- February: Arts Festival, Mount Dora Music Festival, Renninger's Antique Extravaganza
- March: Taste of Mount Dora/Casino Night, Mount Dora Spring Show, Sailboat Regatta, Florida Storytelling Festival
- May: Blues n'Groove Weekend
- July: Independence Day Celebration
- August: Highwaymen Art Show
- October: Bicycle Festival, Craft Fair
- November: Plant & Garden Fair, Scottish Highland Festival, Renninger's Antique Extravaganza, Light Up Mount Dora, Lakes and Hills Garden Club Tour, Art of the Deal
- December: Christmas Parade & Christmas Walk, Christmas Lighted Boat Parade, Christmas Tour of Homes, Children's Christmas in the Park with Snow

The Lakeside Inn

The story of the Lakeside Inn began in 1883 when J.P. and Annie Donnelly partnered with John Alexander and Colonel John McDonald to create the ten-room, two-story Alexander House on the shores of Lake Dora. By 1903, new owner Emma Boone had expanded the hotel and changed its name to the Lakeside Inn. Charles Edgerton and other investors made additional improvements when they purchased the inn in 1925 and were pleased when Calvin Coolidge and his wife, Grace, arrived for a month-long sabbatical in January 1930. In time, Charles's son, Dick Edgerton, took over as owner and manager, a position he'd hold for more than forty years. By the mid-1980s, the aging inn was in danger of being razed before investors stepped in to make major renovations that capitalized on its picturesque setting and preserve its Jazz Age charm. Listed on the National Register of Historic Places in 1987, it continues to be a focal point of the community. For a complete history of one of Mount Dora's most recognized landmarks, read Judy Pendleton's 1998 book *The Lakeside Inn*.

The Inn Crowd

By the early 1990s, bed-and-breakfast inns were becoming a nationwide trend. With Mount Dora's festivals, fairs, antiques and boutiques luring more visitors, lodging was at a premium. Aside from the Lakeside Inn and a few highway hotels, inns would provide the only other accommodations. Ed and Debbie Seabrook were the first to open an inn, the Seabrook Bed & Breakfast on Donnelly Street, and soon other aspiring innkeepers began converting old hotels, apartment houses and vintage homes into B&Bs. Today, nearly a dozen B&Bs have become an integral part of the community, opening their doors and welcoming travelers from across America.

Oldies but Goodies

As Mount Dora's downtown retail sector was coming to life in the 1980s, the popularity of its mom and pop antique shops was gaining a reputation. Sensing a trend, in February 1984 Renninger's Twin Markets set up shop on 117 acres of rolling countryside along Highway 441. Actually, it set up many, many, many shops.

On any given weekend, you'll find approximately 250 dealers at the antique market selling thousands of items from paper goods and rare books to vintage dolls and train sets. There are architectural accents and period home furnishings, signed pottery pieces and fine etched china, as well as wind-up phonographs, handcrafted clocks and just about everything else you can imagine (and countless things you can't). At the top of the hill, Renninger's flea market hosts a few hundred more dealers with farm-fresh produce and cool collectibles mixed in among the flea market merchandise.

With the arrival of Renninger's, Mount Dora became known as the "Antique Capital of Central Florida," and articles in *USA Today*, *Southern Living*, *Country Living* and other publications helped create a new destination for local collectors and weekend visitors. Buying reaches a fever pitch during Antique Extravaganzas, held on the third weekends of November, January and February. That's when nearly 1,500 dealers unload their trailers, pitch their tents and lay out their inventory for three-day treasure hunts. In recent years, Renninger's has introduced special events, including concerts, car shows, garden fairs, music swaps, Civil War reenactments, Native American powwows and other themed weekends.

www.renningers.com

Mount Dora Historic Sites

Across Florida, more than 750 state-approved historical markers combine to tell the state's history. Either denoting a Florida Heritage Landmark, which has state and/or national significance, or a Florida Heritage Site, which indicates local significance, they appear only at sites that have been reviewed by the Florida Division of Historical Resources. Of Mount Dora's historical markers approved by the state, two of the three are associated with the city's African American community. The information here is as it appears on the markers.

Milner-Rosenwald Academy
1560 North Highland Street

Milner-Rosenwald Academy served African-American school children from 1926 to 1962. When fire destroyed the old school in 1922, parents and community leaders, led by Mamie Lee Gilbert (1886–1976) and Lula Butler, raised money for a new one. Seed money came from the Rosenwald Foundation, founded in 1913 by philanthropist Julius Rosenwald (1862–1932) to build black schools in the South. Matching funds came from Rev. Duncan C. Milner (1841–1928), Mount Dora, committed foe of racial injustice. Despite the inequity of segregation, Milner-Rosenwald was a source of community pride. Its graduates were leaders, scholars, writers and contributing members of society. Many today remember favorite teachers and activities—the marching band, the glee club, the Maypole Festival, the state championship girls' basketball team. As enrollment grew, a new Milner-Rosenwald Academy was built, at 1250 Grant Ave. The old academy housed the community's first kindergarten, the East Town branch library, the youth center and, later, the Head Start program. After integration in 1970 the Milner-Rosenwald Academy was renamed Mount Dora Middle School and the name Milner-Rosenwald Academy became a cherished part of Mount Dora's history.

Witherspoon Lodge of Free and Accepted Masons, No. 111
Corner of Grant Avenue and North Clayton Street

The Witherspoon Lodge of Free and Accepted Masons, No. 111, is one of Florida's oldest functioning African American lodges. Established in 1898, it followed the tradition of Prince Hall (1735–1807), who opposed racial oppression in Colonial New England and founded the first African American Lodge in the United States. The Witherspoon Lodge bought this frame vernacular style building in 1903 and has met here since then. Masonic rites require that meetings be held on the second floor. The building also houses the Order of the Eastern Star, the Masonic women's auxiliary. The Masons, the world's largest fraternal organization, are committed to community service, mutual aid and the pursuit of free thought. In Mount Dora, the Witherspoon Lodge has provided help and shelter to various community organizations. In 1922, fire destroyed the city's one-room segregated school for African-American children (Public School No. 66, first established

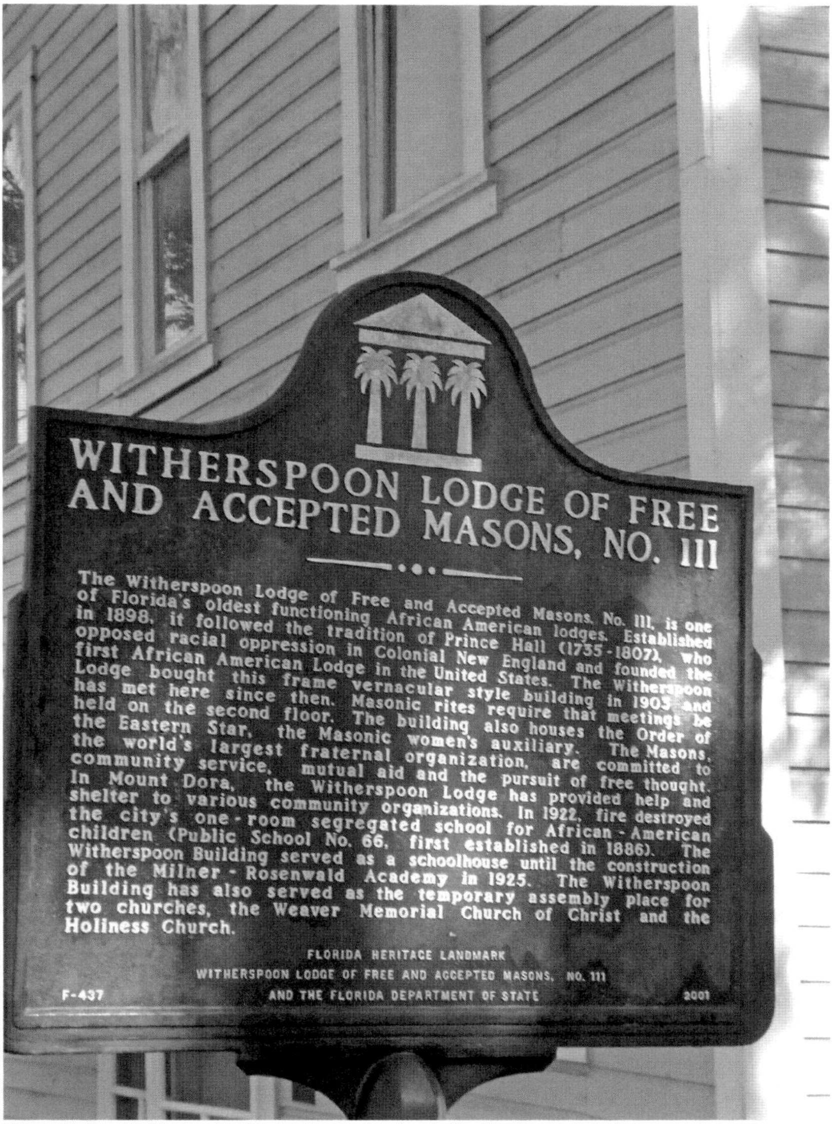

A state historic marker at the Witherspoon Lodge attests to its significance in Mount Dora's history. *Nancy Howell.*

in 1886). The Witherspoon Building served as a schoolhouse until the construction of the Milner-Rosenwald Academy in 1925. The Witherspoon Building has also served as the temporary assembly place for two churches, the Weaver Memorial Church of Christ and the Holiness Church.

Donnelly House
Donnelly Street between Fifth and Sixth Avenues

John P. Donnelly, a native of Pittsburgh, came to Mount Dora in 1879. In 1881, he married Annie McDonald Stone, a prominent landholder in the community. Successful in a number of real estate and business ventures, Donnelly built this imposing Queen Anne–style house in 1893. He was among the founders of the local yacht club and served as the city's first mayor in 1910. In 1924, he sold the land for the park named for his wife, who had died in 1908. He died in 1930. The Donnelly House, now owned by Mount Dora Lodge No. 238, F&AM, was listed in the National Register of Historic Places on April 4, 1975.

Never Were There Such Devoted Sisters

In 1988, a Scottish solicitor expressed interest in pairing the Royal Burgh of Forres, Scotland, with Mount Dora as part of the Sister Cities program. The following year, the Mount Dora Sister Cities Association was formed, and so began a long-lasting friendship.

So, what exactly do the two cities have in common? Like Mount Dora, Forres also has golf courses, bed-and-breakfasts and a lawn bowling club. Each holds numerous festivals throughout the year, and their populations are roughly the same (about thirteen thousand), although the towns were founded centuries apart: Forres in 1140 and Mount Dora in 1910. Notably, in both cities the main highway goes *around* the town rather than through it.

To maintain the person-to-person relationships essential to the program, throughout the year the Mount Dora Sister Cities Association hosts events like the Robert Burns Supper (featuring bagpipes and haggis), a kirking of the tartans and a traditional party called a *ceilidh* ("kay'lee"). Through membership dues, fundraisers and an annual grant from the Mount Dora Community Trust, two Mount Dora High School students are selected to travel to Forres for a full month each summer, fulfilling the program's mission of fostering friendship and understanding between different cultures.

www.mountdorasistercities.com

Community Building 2.0

After producing several events in the aging Mount Dora Community Building, in 2004 the authors recognized that the 1929 Mediterranean Revival venue was in desperate need of a face-lift. Feeling that performers and attendees deserved a first-class auditorium and that the city needed a cultural, educational and economic stimulus, they brought the idea of renovations to the attention of city council.

As other community activists had learned, the key to success was citizen support coupled with city involvement. After presenting a plan for minor aesthetic improvements, they obtained a $2,500 grant from the Community Trust to commission creative renderings. Upon reviewing the drawings, council members authorized $25,000 for first-phase improvements, which included new stage curtains, faux painting, period wall sconces, electrical repairs, plasterwork and stage enhancements.

During renovations, the struggling building revealed that it was in need of far more extensive care. The roof leaked, the walls were crumbling and the air conditioning system drowned out performers. Realizing that only a major restoration could save the venue, the authors sought grassroots community support and formed the 501(c)(3) nonprofit organization Building a Community Performing Arts Center (BACPAC, later the Mount Dora Community Building Foundation). Through benefit concerts, donations and pledges, the BACPAC board raised funds that were donated to the city and demonstrated the community's interest in the project. Major improvements were ready to begin.

Despite setbacks, side issues and a handful of critics who proposed that the building be demolished, city council members realized the importance of the project. In June 2006, they approved $2.7 million for a full renovation and expansion that would transform the venue into a state-of-the-art performance center.

Today, the building stands as a testament to the town and hosts a full calendar of events, fulfilling the original mission statement of the Mount Dora Community Building Foundation: "To enhance the cultural, educational, and economic development of Mount Dora."

Mount Dora Mayors, 1910–2015

J.P. Donnelly
1910–13

Monroe V. Simpson
1913–15

J.H. Crane
1915–17

Dr. O.W. Sadler
1917–21

Adam Hazelwood
1921–23

A.J. Waltz
1923–27

D.C. Sherman
1927–30

Wells E. Lackey
1930–32

George L. Hanscom
1932–33

Monroe V. Simpson
1933–46

J.E. Fortner
1946–50

D. Fletcher Crane
1950–52

Lou L. Heaton
1952–56

W.D. Patton
1956–60

Guy C. Bliss
1960–62

Jesse D. Willmott
1962–74

Thomas R. Champion
1974–77

Jefferson G. Ray III
1977–78

Margaret W. Lofroos
1978–80

Gordon Dake
1980–83

William O. Boyd
1983–87

Jeff Book
1987–90

Robert Wilson
1990–91

Paulette Alexander
1991–2000

James E. Yatsuk
2000–2007

Melissa DeMarco
2007–11

Robert Thielhelm Sr.
2011–13

Catherine T. Hoechst
2013–15

Nick Girone
2015–

I Want to Ride My Bicycle

Started in 1974, the annual Mount Dora Bicycle Festival may not be the Tour de France, but it certainly has become a tradition among riders who choose from among routes ranging from easy (twelve miles) to challenging (one hundred miles). The October event attracts more than one thousand cyclists eager to pedal along country roads and climb graceful hills, although those hills can become overwhelming obstacles near the end of a long ride. The fellowship of other riders, pedaling in the shade of canopy roads and whirring alongside placid lakes are all part of its appeal. Discovering destinations like Sugarloaf Mountain (elevation 312 feet) and the Bavarian-themed Yalaha Bakery combine to make this one of the most popular festivals on the calendar.

The Bicycle Festival is a continuation in a long history of local cycling. In the 1890s, enthusiasts had laid out the first leg of a trail between Mount Dora and Eustis in the hopes that it would be the start of longer trail with side runs to Tavares, Tangerine, Zellwood, Apopka, Orlando, Winter Park and Sanford. Ultimately, from Sanford they envisioned a fifty-mile trail cut across the land taking riders to the Indian River near the Atlantic Ocean. That path was never completed, but closer to home, Mount Dora cyclists were pleased with a then state-of-the-art riding path. As described by a "wheel man" in Longstreet's *History of Mount Dora*: "The method of making the path in this town was to drag a plank with a horse; on the underside of the plank were four little harrow frames two inches thick and 18 inches wide, with sufficient weight on top to remove the grass, weeds, roots, and sand on either side, forging a depressed path 18 inches wide and four inches deep. This path is filled two inches deep with clay, well packed and rolled, and makes a nice path for pedestrians or wheel men."

www.mountdorabicyclefestival.com

No Need to Be Coy, Roy

Like most towns, Mount Dora has had its share of characters, but when it came to scammers, scoundrels, con men and ne'er-do-wells, perhaps no one checked all of these boxes better than Ed Roy.

Roy arrived in 1984 and immediately became one of the most recognizable men in town. In a 2001 *Orlando Sentinel* feature, Ramsey Campbell reported that after Roy amassed a complicated fortune through the sale of solar water heaters in Miami, he bought up most of downtown, including the old Mount Dora Hotel (renaming it Quincy Market), a laundry that became the Baker Street Gallery, a former gas station that became a Mexican restaurant and several other properties, including the Highlander Pool & Tennis Club. For his residence, he purchased the grand home of Lewis R. Heim, who founded and financed Sylvan Shores in the 1920s. Impressing many residents, he also opened the Mount Dora Academy for gifted children, only to see it close after numerous complaints. Within a few years of his arrival, Roy knew that it was time to hit the road. His role in the sale of the solar heaters and misuse of related tax shelters convinced attorneys and federal investigators that he was a criminal mastermind and the "consummate con man" who, according to the *Sentinel*, ripped off investors for $30 million, evaded corporate taxes of $20 million and stashed away millions more.

After leaving Mount Dora with vacant properties and a trail of confusion, he eventually ended up on the lam in Canada to avoid federal tax fraud and obstruction of justice charges. Roy denied the allegations and claimed that he was the victim of a vendetta by the country sheriff. Although some of his associates would serve time after pleading guilty, in the end Roy would play out the clock in Canada and never see the inside of a prison.

Back in Mount Dora, whether it was the old Mount Dora Hotel or the former home of Lewis R. Heim, buyers would spend months, or often years, trying to gain clear title to the properties that had been mired in the many frauds of Ed Roy.

The Castle on the Hill

In the 1930s, builder and designer Arthur Frothingham chose Mount Dora as his home. The man who claimed a distant kinship to Washington Irving moved from Sleepy Hollow, New York, and began work on the twenty-two-room Castle on the Hill. Unfortunately, Frothingham died during the home's construction, which left it available for George Malone to sell to Mount Dora's first celebrity resident: Napoleon Hill. Having written the stories of successful people as a reporter, Hill's own fame came as author of motivational books, including *The Law of Success* (1928), *The Magic Ladder to Success* (1930) and his blockbuster *Think and Grow Rich* (1937), which to date has sold more than 70 million copies.

Napoleon and Annie Lou Hill arrived in 1938 and, after several years in Mount Dora, would spend their final years in South Carolina. In 1973, the Castle on the Hill, arguably the most recognized home next to the Donnelly House, was razed and replaced by condominiums.

It's Showtime!

Back in September 1948 at the Community Building, a group of keenly interested residents listened to Gordon Goodrich share his thoughts on the beauty of live theater. There that evening was Celia Claflin. "He spoke so glowingly of all the attributes of live theater," she recalled. "What it could do for our community and for each of us as well, that we were carried away and that very night elected officers."

In a scene reminiscent of a Mickey Rooney and Judy Garland film, Claflin was elected president and Goodrich took on the role of director, and the group—which also included William Barker and his son Bill, Walter Patton, Mae Buckman and Guyla Bissell—decided to open a theater. Aware of an abandoned building on Charles Street that had served as a youth center, citrus packinghouse and ice storage plant, the group raised funds from citizens and local businesses to cover the $100 monthly rent. Next they found chairs from an old Tavares high school, used dynamite to blast down 22-inch-thick walls to create a proscenium

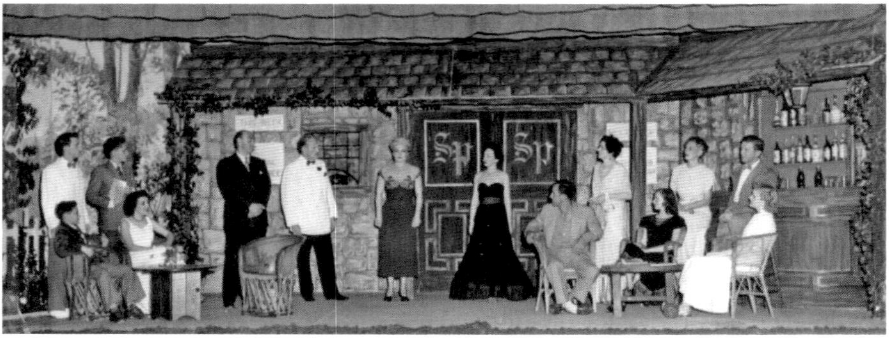

Just months after deciding to bring live theater to Mount Dora, founders of the IceHouse Theatre located and renovated a venue, rehearsed and then took to the stage in their 1949 premiere. *IceHouse Theatre.*

arch and then detonated more TNT to disintegrate a portion of the loading platform to create a stage.

For the newly named IceHouse Players to keep their dream afloat, they held bingo games, dances and rummage sales. Mary Dopkeen, who owned Sally Dress Shop as well as several parcels of land, was so impressed by their passion and enthusiasm that she offered a valuable downtown lot for the Players to auction. While tempted, they declined her generous offer in favor of a Sally Dress Shop–sponsored fashion show and raffle.

The following February, the local actors made their debut before a full house in *Return Engagement.* A success from the start, the troupe returned to that stage for ten years before the city donated land on Unser Street, where a new 270-seat theater opened in the fall of 1958. After more than a half century of performances, donors led by the Sonnentag Foundation and Clarence and Chris Kolek financed a major renovation in 2011. Perhaps the most generous donation, however, has been the contribution of time and talent offered by generations of actors, ushers, musicians, dancers, directors, production staff and volunteers who have made the IceHouse Theatre an essential part of the community.

www.icehousetheatre.com

When the Trains Come

Prior to Chautauqua's premiere season in 1887, a line that ran from Sanford to Tavares was modified to include morning and evening stops in Mount Dora. Later, a siding was added parallel to the track, allowing for freight cars to load and unload. By 1915, the Atlantic Coast Line Railroad had invested $8,223 to build a new station to accommodate passengers. Within a few years, four trains a day were pulling in and heading out of the station carrying passengers and freight. When automobiles nudged trains out of favor, passenger service ceased in 1950. In 1973, freight cars made their last scheduled run, although some local carriers still use the tracks. Signing a lease with the Seaboard Coast Line for $1 per year, the empty station was recycled into its present use as the Mount Dora Area Chamber of Commerce. In 1992, the station was placed on the National Register of Historic Places.

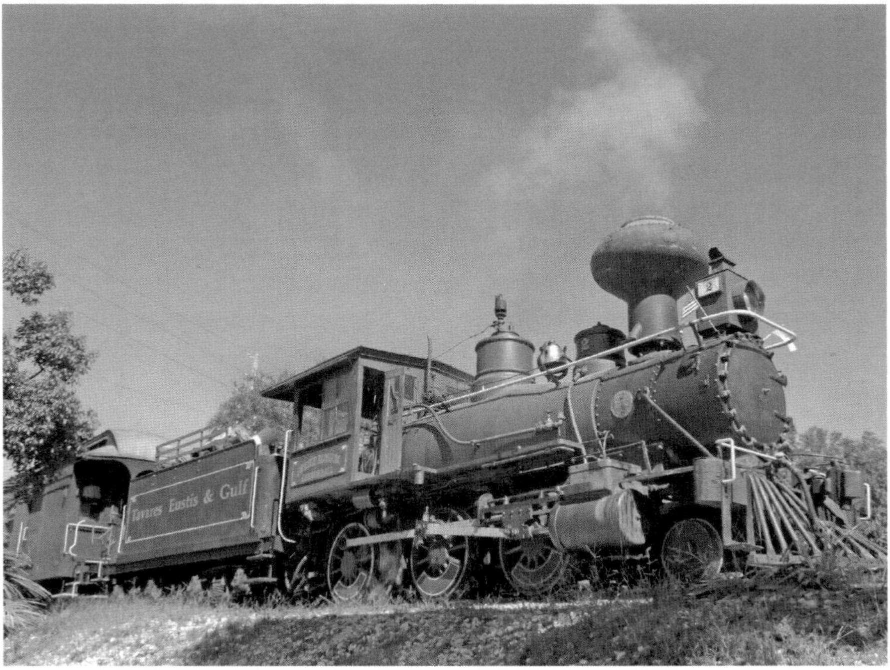

Reflecting the glory days of steam locomotion that helped open Mount Dora to visitors and new residents, a vintage steam train still rides the same rails. *Nancy Howell.*

On a Roll: The Mount Dora Lawn Bowling Club

When members of the Mount Dora Lawn Bowling Club are on the rinks in their crisp white uniforms during tournament play, it is one of the most pleasant sights in Mount Dora, as well as the reflection of a tradition that began in the 1920s.

Winter residents who attended a tournament in St. Petersburg brought the idea back to Mount Dora. Presenting their vision of a lawn bowling club to the city council, they reasoned that the investment in rinks would pay for itself with an increase in tourist traffic—more visitors meant more disposable income deposited in local cash registers. Whether members of

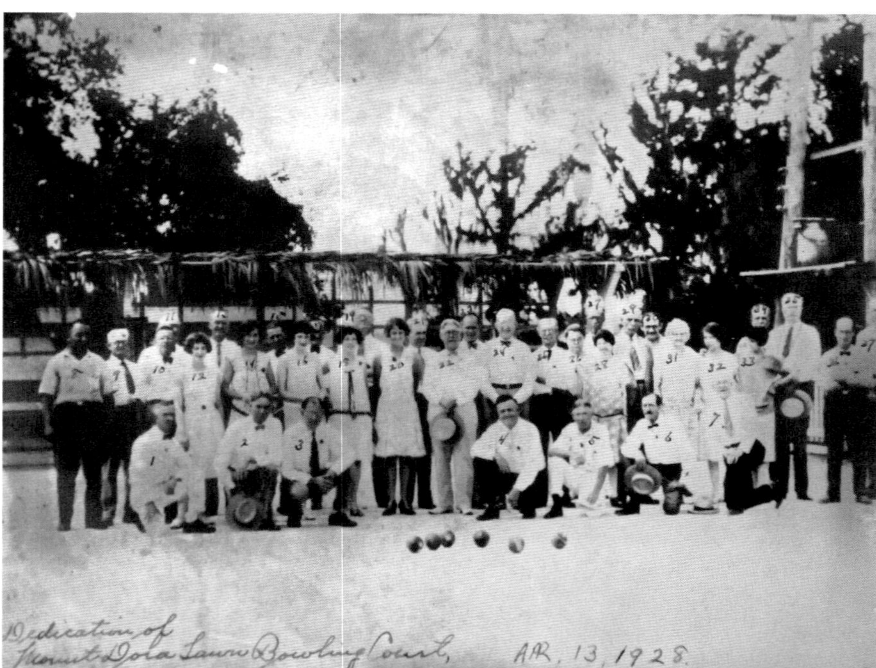

Refined, relaxing and recreational, lawn bowling has been part of Mount Dora since its debut. Shown on opening day in 1928, these players would be pleased that the sport has retained its popularity nearly a century later. *Mount Dora Historical Society.*

the city council actually believed this or not is anyone's guess, but by April 1928, rinks had been installed at the south end of Donnelly Street just steps from the Lakeside Inn and play commenced. The first match pitted Mount Dora against a visiting team from Orlando, and soon after, members of the Mount Dora Lawn Bowling Club were competing in international matches, as teams from Great Britain arrived to test the skills of local players.

A sport that members says "takes a day to learn and a lifetime to master" has been a welcome part of the community for nearly a century, and residents show no sign of stopping. According to a club history prepared by historian (and lawn bowler) James Laux, with nearly three hundred members, the Mount Dora Lawn Bowling Club is the largest Bowls USA–affiliated club in America.

www.mountdoralawnbowling.com

Glimpses of Mount Dora

In a 1916 promotional brochure for Mount Dora, an enthusiastic local poet wrote an ode to his or her fair city under the title "Glimpses of Mount Dora." If that unknown person thought enough to compose this piece, it's only fitting that, a century later, it should close out this volume:

Sweet Southern airs and flowery blooms
Of the magnolia's rare perfumes,
The breath of rose, the violet's scent,
Is one commingled sweetness blent,
Entrance me as I muse of thee,
Fair Florida, far down the sea.
We sing thy grace fair land of flowers,
Thy lakes of blue, thy emerald bowers
Thy perfumes, borne on every breeze.
Thy tints from far Hesperides.
We laud thy joy, we boast thy charms.
Thy whispering pines, thy rustling p'ams.
And spread the robe of love anew,
For dainty feet mid flowers and dew.

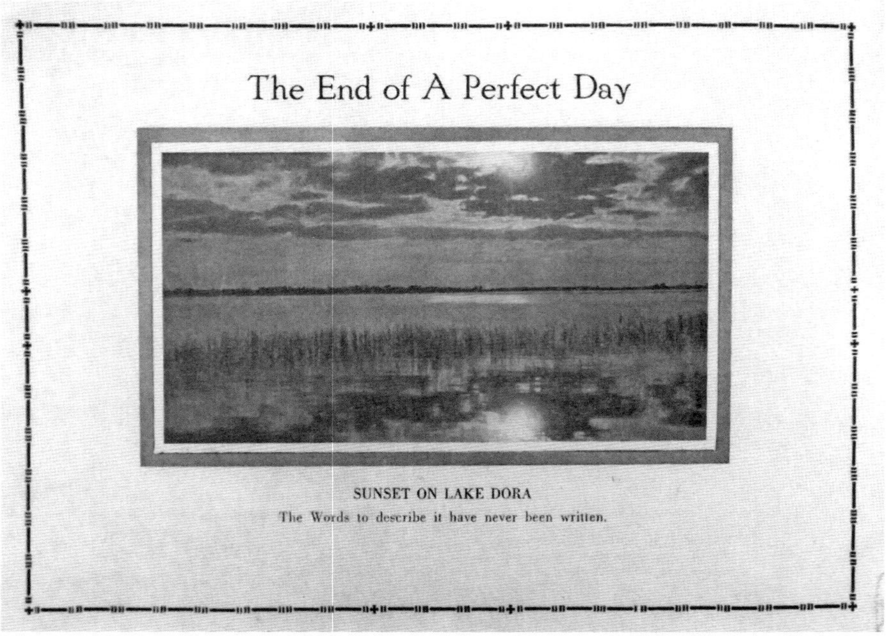

A fitting end in 1916…and today. *Mount Dora Historical Society.*

SOURCES

Burley, Eugene, Reverend. *Mount Dora: The Rest of the Story, Plus!* N.p.: Displays for Schools, 2000.

Edgerton, David. *Memories of Mount Dora and Lake County: 1845 to 1981*. N.p., 1983.

Lake County Historical Society Collection, Tavares, Florida.

Laux, James. *A Short History of Mount Dora, Florida.* N.p.: Firstpublish Inc., 2001.

Longstreet, R.J. *The Story of Mount Dora, Florida*. N.p., 1960.

Mount Dora Citizen. www.mountdoracitizen.com.

Mount Dora Historical Society Collection. Available at the W.T. Bland Public Library, Mount Dora, Florida.

Mount Dora Topic Collection. Available at the Eustis Memorial Library, Eustis, Florida.

Orlando Sentinel, Lake County edition.

Owens, Vivian. *The Mount Dorans*. N.p., Eschar Publications, 2001.

Pendleton, Judy. *The Lakeside Inn.* N.p., 1998.

INDEX

ABOUT THE AUTHORS

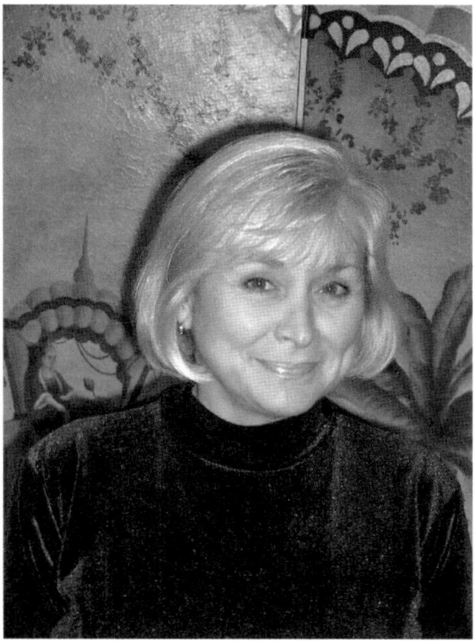

Nancy Howell is a former television producer, writer and on-air personality who currently owns and operates the Coconut Cottage Inn Bed and Breakfast. She is also co-owner of Mount Dora Productions with husband, Gary McKechnie, and has served as the executive director of the Mount Dora Music Festival since 2005. For the past ten years, she has worked as a Florida State Supreme Court–certified mediator for the Lake County Court of the Fifth Judicial Circuit. Since moving to Mount Dora in 1992, her volunteer service on boards and committees has included Lake County Economic Development and Tourism, the Mount Dora Area Chamber of Commerce, the Mount Dora Village Merchants and Business Association, the Festival Alliance, Lights of Lake, the Mount Dora Lodging Association, Mount Dora Public Safety, Mount Dora Historic Preservation, the Mount Dora Historical Society, the Building a Performing Arts Center and the Mount Dora Community Building Foundation, among others. She is credited with reestablishing the Old-Fashioned Fourth of July Celebration, creating A Taste of Mount Dora, enhancing the Mount Dora Light Up holiday celebration and producing the Mount Dora Chautauqua in conjunction with the Florida Humanities Council.

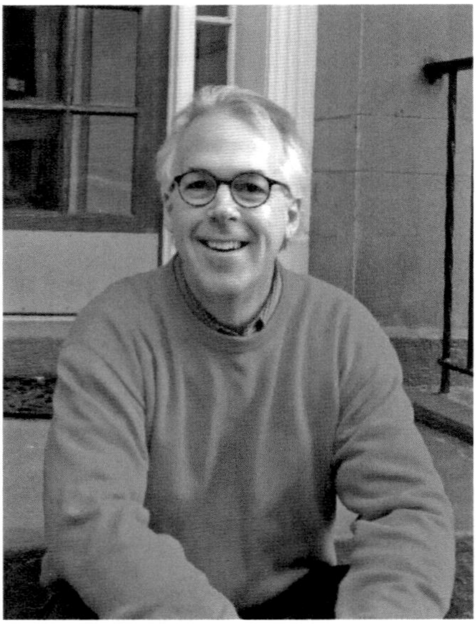

Gary McKechnie is a former stand-up comedian, improv actor and author of the nation's best-selling motorcycle guidebook, *Great American Motorcycle Tours*. He is a two-time *National Geographic* author (*USA 101* and *Ten Best of Everything: National Parks*) and has written for Walt Disney World, Fodor's, Harley-Davidson, Rand McNally, AOL, *People*, *National Geographic Traveler*, the *Washington Post*, the *Chicago Tribune*, the *Atlanta Constitution*, the *Orlando Sentinel*, the *Miami Herald*, *Orlando* magazine, *Florida* magazine and United Airlines' *Hemispheres*. He is a two-time winner of the Lowell Thomas Travel Journalism Award and a member of the Society of America Travel Writers and, for four years, was Visit Florida's "Off the Beaten Path" Insider. In 2014, he was selected by the Motorcycle Industry Council to travel across America to ride, write and report on the Cannon Ball Centennial Ride, a 3,450-mile cross-country motorcycle expedition. He lectures on American travel, culture and music aboard the *Queen Mary 2*, the *Queen Victoria* and the ships of the Seabourn and Silversea lines. In 2003, he initiated and then led the drive to renovate the Mount Dora Community Building and created the 501(c)(3) nonprofit Mount Dora Community Building Foundation to aid in its operation.

www.garymckechnie.com